Fabulous Food

SEXY RECIPES FOR HEALTHY LIVING

Fabulous Food

SEXY RECIPES FOR HEALTHY LIVING

Sophie Michell

sphere

SPHERE

I want to say thanks to some important contributors to this book: Sian and
Emil at D.R.ink for their brilliant design work; Maria Merola for lending
me beautiful jewellery; thanks to Giuseppe Zanotti and Kyri dresses; to
Daniel Galvin; to Agnieszka Hancock for letting us use her beautiful
home; to Mary-Anna Kearney for her styling and to Michelle Foxley for
her skills with hair and make-up.

First published in Great Britain in 2008 by Sphere

Copyright © Sophie Michell 2008

Design by D.R. ink
Photos of Sophie Michell by John Swanell
Food photography Chris Alack
Food stylist Kim Morphew
Prop stylist Sue Radcliffe
Home economist Roz Denny

A CIP catalogue record for this book
is available from the British Library.

ISBN 978-1-84744-211-6

Printed and bound in Italy

Sphere
An imprint of
Little, Brown Book Group
100 Victoria Embankment
London EC4Y 0DY

An Hachette Livre UK Company
www.hachettelivre.co.uk

www.littlebrown.co.uk

Foreword

Food is always something to get excited about as it can bring so much pleasure, but the usual foods and recipes aimed at health-conscious people take the joy out of eating along with the calorie content – not to mention the loss in flavour! In *Fabulous Food* Sophie has combined her skills as a trained chef with her desire to look and feel her best and the results mean that you can enjoy wonderful food very easily. Finding food that's light but still delicious is difficult, and this is where Sophie excels. After all, if you want to watch your weight then this shouldn't mean that you can't enjoy fantastic food sensations or find the perfect meal for every occasion.

In my experience of working with Sophie I've come to appreciate her passion for good food and her ability to cook creatively. When we last worked together we each made a traditional French dish but Sophie made an alternative recipe based on the original which stayed true to her particular approach to cooking. While I was dubious when she dispensed with the lovely cream and cheese from the recipe's usual ingredients, I think there is always room for alternative recipes and was really impressed with the substitutions she made and the way the finished dish turned out. I love her cooking philosophy that runs through this book and her clever ways of adapting her dishes so that they are lighter but still as delicious as any full-fat version. I'm sure you will enjoy the way that these recipes are original, fresh, and even indulgent and sensuous.

Jean Christophe Novelli

Toby Meritt

 Acknowledgements

It's a great privilege to have a book coming out. The past few months have been a whirlwind and it has only been made possible by a lot of special people.

I want to say thank you to my mother Chris Michell, for being the original driving force behind my career and for looking after me so well. Thank you to my step-father John Heath for believing in me. Thanks to my maternal grandparents for doting on me from day one and to my darling little brother. I also want to say a little thank you to my love, RR: your kisses kept me smiling while I was writing.

A big thanks goes to Jaine Brent, my agent, for getting the deal. This book is very important to me and has been put together by the brilliant team at Little, Brown. Huge thanks to my editor Sarah Rustin: we got there in the end! Thanks, too, to Kirsteen Astor and Caroline Hogg for all their efforts. Thanks to John Swanell for always taking good photos of me; Chris and Sue for surpassing all possible expectations on making the food look so beautiful; Roz Denny for all her hard work; and to everyone else involved, I can't name you all but I include you here.

Finally, I am dedicating this book to my brother Thomas Edwin Michell, who passed away as a baby. We all miss you and the amazing person you would have become. I hope I am making you proud and I wish you were still here.

Contents

Introduction   9

Home Time   12

- QUICK FIXES FOR EVERY DAY OF THE WEEK
- STORE CUPBOARD AND FREEZER SPECIALS
- EASY PACKED LUNCHES

Guilt-Free Comfort Food   46

- SAVOURY COMFORT FOOD WITHOUT THE GUILT
- NOT-SO-NAUGHTY SWEET TREATS FOR THE TIMES WHEN NOTHING ELSE WILL DO
- IN-A-FLASH HEALTHY SNACKS

Social Butterfly   78

- GLAMOROUS LIGHT-BITE CANAPÉS
- SLEEK AND SLENDER DINNER PARTY DISHES
- PRE-PARTY STOMACH LINERS
- LOW CALORIE COCKTAILS
- HEARTY HEALTHY HANGOVER CURES
- BRUNCH IDEAS
- AFTERNOON TEA DELIGHTS

Turn Up the Heat   154

- APHRODISIAC DINNERS – IRRESISTIBLE LIGHT MEALS TO SEDUCE THAT CERTAIN SOMEONE
- CHEEKY MORSELS TO KEEP YOUR ENERGY UP
- MEALS TO IMPRESS YOUR FAMILY … OR HIS

Quick Fixes to fit into that Little Black Dress or Bikini   176

- ONE-WEEK COUNTDOWN TILL THAT SPECIAL OCCASION
- TOO-MUCH-PARTYING DETOX FOOD
- RECIPES FOR DIETARY RESTRICTIONS

The Glamorous Gourmet Tricks of the Trade   202

- BASIC CLASSIC RECIPES
- HOW TO SHOP
- FOOD WARDROBE
- FRIDGE SAVERS
- DRESSING UP YOUR TABLE
- GREAT SHOPS AND SUPPLIERS

Introduction

Today's women try to do everything, from juggling a pressured job to running a home, not to mention being a doting girlfriend/mother/wife/feisty singleton, and all while trying to walk in six-inch heels and squeeze into the latest fashion in size minus-one (OK, so minus-one doesn't exist, but give it time!). Never has life been such a fast-paced balancing act, and that's before we even step foot in the kitchen. Feeling tired yet?

Well, it's time to sit down with a glass of wine, heave a sigh of relief and let me show you the tricks of the trade that will provide you with delicious, stylish and healthy recipes for every occasion. They'll make your life so much easier, leaving you time to get on with being effortlessly glamorous.

At your fingertips are the best quick-fix dinners for the end of a busy day at work – even for times when your fridge is empty and you're relying on the store cupboard for a tasty meal. There's comfort food that won't pile on the pounds, fabulous party food and professional-looking canapés which can be made in between applying your mascara and painting your nails. There are also aphrodisiac meals to cook for that special someone which will satiate your appetite but won't weigh you down or leave you feeling bloated – especially when you want to be at your slinkiest and sexiest. And then there are recipes for those daunting family occasions, whether it's cooking for your mother . . . or that special someone's mother (if it gets that far!).

From great meals to cook for yourself for any mood or occasion, to stress-free but impressive meals to cook for your family or friends, I've taken care of the healthy eating issue which means you can enjoy the delights of food without any awful feelings of guilt – a feeling that I believe should never be associated with the joy of eating. I'll also show you how to make the most of your

ingredients by using any that are left over in other recipes throughout the book, so nothing gets wasted – just more fabulous food for you instead!

I love food and cooking. I believe that our diet is at the core of our health and happiness, and that when you've mastered food, everything else should fall into place. I make mistakes like everyone else, but there is always a dish that will make things better! I suffered from ME as a teenager and though I recovered quickly the first time around, at nineteen I had a relapse. Having started in a professional kitchen at fourteen, worked my way up in some of London's top restaurants and catered for some of the capital's most famous residents, I had always loved food (I became a chef so that I could eat more!), but I found myself gaining weight. As much I told myself, 'Never trust a skinny chef' and, 'Food is my life', I wasn't looking or feeling great and I was spending too much time in doctors' surgeries. After seeing several specialists I was told to give up wheat, sugar and coffee (my consistent companion), along with many other foods. This got me thinking about what I was putting into my body. I looked at all the diet and healthy-eating books on the market but they left me feeling worse! They were all based on deprivation, and living only on raw food or a daily torture of mung bean stew is not my idea of living at all! So I adapted my own balanced way of eating.

'Diet' is still a swear word to me, but I now know how to create gorgeous food by eliminating the ingredients that don't agree with me. I've since lost at least two stone and I am at a happy medium (although depending on mood and stress level, I can vary a few pounds here and there!). And if I do occasionally want to indulge, it will be only with the highest quality ingredients and with recipes where I can make substitutions for healthier foods instead of carbs, butter or cream. While there's no point kidding ourselves that there's such a thing as a healthy pudding, my desserts and cakes are at least healthier than ordinary options.

This book is devoted to looking and feeling fab, and whether you're naturally a size eight or sixteen, these recipes will bring simplicity and sparkle to your life and help you in every situation: from mending a broken heart (without diving for the cream buns!) to throwing the most talked-about party in town. So pop on your highest heels, slick on your lip gloss and let's get cooking.

Sophie Michell

Home Time

QUICK FIXES FOR EVERY DAY OF THE WEEK

Your home should be your haven, somewhere that you can escape from everything and relax. Home is where you should feel safe, happy and comfortable. Sometimes, it can feel like I never see the inside of my house, and with work and social commitments it can be the last place on my mind. I can tell when life is getting on top of me and when I need to slow down – it's when I feel like there has been a clothes explosion in my house, and I can barely get out of the door for shoes and dresses! **Still, food is my solace**, so I will always find the time to cook (despite my hatred of washing up, there is nothing glam about that).

The key is to finding quick-fix meals that will **fill your kitchen with homely, warming smells** and your belly full of good food. Saying that, I am a sucker for beautiful flowers and expensive scented candles (boys, if you're reading this, now you know!). If the budget allows, these also help with the homely vibe.

Mackerel with garlic sauce and apple and walnut salad

I'm always waxing lyrical about Greek food as I think it gets a bad press. People only think of deep-fried calamari and kebabs, but there is so much more to Greece than that. This garlic sauce is called skordalia and is often used as a dip. I've paired the sauce with mackerel, as it cuts through the richness of the fish, and added apples and walnuts to give the dish texture. It's also a beautiful dish, with the fuchsia-pink beetroot juices mingling with the snowy-white sauce.

People only think of deep-fried calamari and kebabs, but there is so much more to Greece than that

Serves 2
Preparation time 15 minutes
Cooking time 20 minutes

4 mackerel fillets, about 120g each
1 green apple, quartered, cored and chopped
2 cooked beetroots (without vinegar if possible)
1 tbsp walnuts, roughly chopped
Wild rocket and curly endive (frisee), to serve

For the garlic sauce
1 medium potato, about 200g
3 cloves garlic, crushed
1 tsp sea salt
1 tbsp white wine vinegar
3 tbsp olive oil
Juice ½ lemon

Firstly, make the garlic sauce. Peel and cube the potato, place in a saucepan and cover with water. Bring to the boil and then turn down to simmer for about 12 minutes until cooked. Drain and mash.

Preheat the grill. Add the garlic to the salt, then mix into the potatoes with the vinegar, oil and lemon juice. Set aside. Chop the beetroot into similar-sized pieces as the apple. Season the mackerel and then grill for about 3 minutes on each side.

To serve, place a handful of rocket and endive salad on each plate, top with the mackerel fillets and then add a dollop of the garlic sauce on the side. Finally, sprinkle the apple, beetroot and walnuts over the garlic sauce and serve.

Five-spice pork chops with garlicky greens

I love Chinese roast pork – the star anise-scented sweet-and-savoury taste is fantastic. When I was a child, Char Sui buns were a firm favourite and I still love gawping at the rows of ducks and lurid pink roasted pork hanging in the windows of Chinese kitchens. This is a quick and easy interpretation of Chinese roasted pork, minus the food dye some people use. The pork only takes a few minutes to marinate and the whole dish takes just fifteen minutes to put together. Even quicker than ordering from the local takeaway! Lovely with plain boiled jasmine Thai or basmati rice.

Fifteen minutes to put together. Even quicker than ordering from the local takeaway!

Serves 2
Preparation time 10 minutes, plus marinating
Cooking time 15 minutes

2 medium-size boneless pork chops, about 150g each
2 heads bok choi (or ½ head of Chinese cabbage, core removed)
1 tbsp sunflower or groundnut oil, for frying
2 cloves garlic, thinly sliced
Pinch dried chilli
About 1 tbsp soy sauce

For the marinade
2–3cm piece ginger
2 tsp Chinese five-spice powder
1 tbsp light soy sauce
1 tbsp honey
1 tsp sesame oil

Firstly, prepare the marinade. Cut the ginger into julienne (thin) strips and then mix together with the rest of the marinade ingredients. Place the pork chops into a shallow dish and pour over the marinade, get your hands in, turn the chops over and make sure they are covered and the marinade is rubbed in, all over. I know this isn't good for the manicure, but sometimes a girl needs to get her hands dirty. Marinate for 5–10 minutes (you can marinate overnight for a deeper flavour, if you have the time).

Heat a grill or non-stick griddle pan until hot and cook the pork for about 6 minutes on each side, basting with the leftover marinade while cooking.

As the pork is cooking, cut the bok choi into quarters or coarsely shred the cabbage. Gently heat a wok to medium heat, add the oil and stir-fry the garlic and chilli for a few seconds (making sure not to burn the garlic), then add the greens and continue to stir-fry for 3 minutes until wilted. Mix in the soy sauce, adding a small splash of water if getting too dry, then stir-fry for a further 3 minutes. Remove from the heat and divide between two warmed plates.

 Turn to page 109 for another recipe using Chinese five-spice

Grilled rib-eye with chimchurri dressing

There are those nights when you just can't beat steak and frites — but you don't exactly want to pile on the pounds that come with deep-fried potatoes and creamy garlic butter. Rib-eye is a fantastically flavoursome cut (just make sure to trim off the fat) and the deep-orange sweet potatoes with the fresh herby dressing are the perfect accompaniment. The dressing goes well with all meat and fish, and makes a great marinade, so make a big batch and use it for chargrilled prawns or chicken tomorrow!

Rib-eye is a fantastically flavoursome cut

Serves 2
Preparation time   15 minutes
Cooking time   55 minutes

1 large sweet potato
About 4 tbsp olive oil
2 rib-eye steaks, about 200g each
100g baby leaf spinach
Sea salt and freshly ground black pepper

For the dressing
1 red chilli, slit and deseeded
1 fat clove garlic
Small handful fresh coriander leaves
Small handful fresh flat-leaf parsley
Juice 1 lime

Preheat the oven to 200°C, Gas Mark 6. Wash and cut the potato into wedges, pat dry with a paper towel then toss in a bowl with a tablespoon of oil. Season and tip out on to a baking dish. Bake for up to 40 minutes until softened.

Meanwhile, make the dressing. Finely chop the chilli, garlic and herbs. Mix with the lime juice and remaining olive oil, then season and set aside.

Heat a non-stick griddle pan until very hot. Season the steaks and grill for 3 minutes on each side for rare steaks, 4 minutes each side for medium. Remove from the heat and rest for 5 minutes.

Wilt the spinach in a pan with a splash of water and seasoning on a medium heat. Drain off any excess water and divide between two warmed dinner plates. Sit the steaks on top and spoon over the dressing. Serve with the potato wedges.

Turn to pages 58, 168–9 and 179 for more recipes using sweet potato

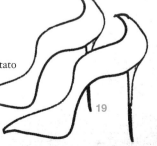

My big, fat Greek burger

In Greece we're lucky enough to be able to go to the butcher's and get him to mince a good piece of lamb or beef, with just the right measure of fat and no gristle. It does take me a lot of hand gestures and pointing to pictures as my Greek is terrible, but we get there in the end and the result is fantastic. If you can get to a butcher, it is SO worth it.

Serves 4
Preparation time   15 minutes
Cooking time   30 minutes

500g lean lamb or beef mince
1 shallot, finely diced
1 clove garlic, crushed
¼ tsp cinnamon
¼ tsp ground cumin
½ tsp dried oregano
100g half-fat feta cheese, crumbled
1 free-range egg yolk, beaten
4 Granary rolls, slit in half (or use wholemeal pittas, slit open)
1 Little Gem lettuce, leaves separated
1–2 medium cooked beetroots, sliced
Sea salt and freshly ground black pepper

For the tzatziki salad
½ cucumber
200g 0% fat Greek yogurt
Small handful fresh mint leaves, chopped
1 clove garlic, crushed

For the tomato relish (optional)
1 shallot, finely chopped
1 clove garlic, crushed
½ red chilli, slit, deseeded and chopped
200g canned chopped tomatoes
1 tbsp white wine vinegar
1 tbsp sultanas
1 tsp fruit sugar, such as fructose

Firstly, to make the tomato relish, take a small heavy-based saucepan and add all the relish ingredients. Bring to the boil, turn down and simmer for 20 minutes or until reduced by half, then leave to cool.

To make the tzatziki, peel the cucumber then halve lengthways and scoop out the seeds with a teaspoon. Slice thinly on the diagonal and tip into a colander. Sprinkle lightly with salt, rub well together and leave for 5 minutes to drain and soften, then rinse well under cold water and pat dry with a paper towel. Mix with the yogurt, mint and garlic. Set aside.

For the burgers, mix together the mince, shallot, garlic, spices, herbs, feta and egg yolk and shape into four neat, even-sized burgers. Heat a heavy-based non-stick frying pan until very hot. Cook the burgers for about 3–4 minutes each side (depending on whether you like them rare or medium rare) until they feel firm but still a little springy and juicy. Remove and leave them to stand for 5 minutes while you warm the baps or pittas.

Layer the ingredients on to four of the roll halves. Start with a lettuce leaf, then a spoonful of tomato relish, then the burger, beetroot slices and finally a dollop of tzatziki. Press on the top of the toasted bun. Get your chops around that!

Asian crab omelette

I'm in love with the balance of flavours essential to Asian food. The combination of sweet, salty and sour just does it for me. The way the flavours have such clarity and unison was a revelation when I first hit the shores of South East Asia, aged eleven. I love the way food is wrapped and rolled up in rice paper or lettuce; food is always fun when you have to use your hands and get stuck in.

In this dish, the omelette is the 'wrapper' and it's great for supper, lunch or an indulgent brunch. Plus, it's a fantastic high-protein meal.

Food is always fun when you have to use your hands and get stuck in

Serves 2
Preparation time   15 minutes
Cooking time   15 minutes

4 free-range eggs
2 tbsp milk
1 red chilli, slit and deseeded
1 clove garlic
3 spring onions
1 tbsp sesame oil
3cm piece fresh ginger, grated
1 tsp curry powder
150g white crab meat
Small handful fresh coriander
2 tbsp vegetable oil
2 tbsp oyster sauce
Pinch toasted sesame seeds
Sea salt and freshly ground black pepper

Whisk together the eggs and milk, and season with salt and pepper. Then finely chop the chilli, garlic and spring onions and fry in the sesame oil with the ginger for about 3 minutes until softened. Season, then add the crab and curry powder. Heat to warm through, then mix in the coriander and set aside.

Take a non-stick omelette pan and heat up half the vegetable oil. Fry half the egg mixture over a medium to low heat, shaking the pan a few times to make a thin omelette. When cooked, transfer to a plate and keep warm, then repeat with the rest of the egg mixture to make a second omelette. To serve, divide the crab mixture between the two omelettes, roll up each one, drizzle with the oyster sauce and sprinkle with the sesame seeds.

Venison steaks with blueberry and sloe gin sauce

Venison is just about one of the best meats you can eat. It's slightly higher in iron than beef and lower in cholesterol than chicken. I adore the flavour of venison and it would be great to see people enjoying it more often. It's available now in most supermarkets.

I've made a quick, glossy, slightly sweet sauce, balanced with an earthy-flavoured celeriac mash. Celeriac is a great vegetable: you could almost pass it off as potato (which is useful for feeding awkward kids and men alike) and your girlfriends will love you as it's lighter than traditional creamy mash.

Venison is just about one of the best meats you can eat

Serves 2
Preparation time 15 minutes
Cooking time 20 minutes

1 small celeriac, about 500g, peeled and cubed
300ml milk
25g butter
2 thick venison loin steaks, about 150g each
1 tbsp olive oil
Sea salt and freshly ground black pepper

For the blueberry sauce
100ml sloe gin
100ml red wine
200g blueberries
2 tbsp redcurrant jelly

Preheat the oven to a very low heat. Put the celeriac in a saucepan and cover with the milk and 300ml water. Add a pinch of salt and bring to the boil. Simmer for 20 minutes or until tender. Drain and mash with the butter, then taste to check the seasoning. Keep warm at a very low oven setting.

Season the venison steaks with salt and pepper. Heat a frying pan until hot, add a tablespoon of oil and sear the steaks for about 3 minutes on each side, or until cooked to your liking. Remove, cover and keep warm in the oven while you make the blueberry sauce.

Deglaze the venison pan by adding the sloe gin and red wine and, over a medium heat, letting the juices bubble up – loosen any sediment in the pan with a flat wooden spatula. Add the blueberries and cook for a few minutes to soften. Stir in the redcurrant jelly and carry on cooking until the sauce reduces by half and the berries continue to soften.

Serve the venison steaks with the blueberry sauce and celeriac mash. This dish goes well with a mound of buttered greens.

Turn to pages 68-9, 139 and 151 for more recipes using blueberries

Parma ham stuffed pork on peas, broad beans and truffle

Pork fillet is an underused cut that is tender, low in fat and very affordable. It can be dressed up in lots of different ways and looks great on the plate – it's also my cheap dinner party special.

Here I've stuffed the fillet with naughtily indulgent truffle paste and aromatic herbs. Because it's so low in fat, you can afford to add a little fat in different areas, so I've wrapped the fillet in Parma ham. This makes it a prettier dish and adds a lot of flavour. Broad beans always seem a rather hard-core vegetable, but when peeled they take on a new delicate persona and are definitely worth the extra work.

It's also my cheap dinner party special

Serves 4
Preparation time   15 minutes
Cooking time   20 minutes

1 tbsp finely chopped fresh sage
1 tbsp finely chopped fresh parsley
2 garlic cloves, finely chopped
1 tsp truffle paste
3–4 tbsp olive oil
2 pork tenderloins, about 250g each, trimmed of fat and membrane
6/8 slices Parma ham, fat stripped off
250g frozen broad beans, thawed
250g frozen petits pois, thawed
Juice 1 lemon
1 tsp chopped mint
75g truffle Pecorino cheese shavings
(or use regular Pecorino or Parmesan if this isn't available)
Sea salt and freshly ground black pepper

Mix together the finely chopped herbs, garlic, truffle paste, 1 tbsp olive oil and a little seasoning. Make an incision halfway along the length of each pork fillet. Fill the incisions with the herb and truffle mixture, rubbing some on the outside of the fillet as well.

Shape into rolls, then wrap each fillet neatly in Parma ham, using 2/4 slices per fillet (you may need slightly less or more Parma ham, depending on how long the fillet is). Make sure you cover the whole of each fillet. Cut them in half to make 4 pieces in total.

Preheat the oven to 190°C, Gas Mark 5. Heat up a large frying pan, add 1–2 tbsp of oil and lightly brown each pork fillet. Then place on a baking tray and put in the oven for 15–20 minutes until just firm when pressed.

While this is cooking, very gently heat the beans and peas with a little lemon juice and olive oil in a saucepan. Season and add the mint.

Serve the pork fillet slices with beans and peas and sprinkle with the truffle Pecorino shavings.

 Turn to page 166 for another recipe using Parma ham

Scallop and shrimp tacos

This is my lighter take on a Florida favourite that uses cornmeal and tacos, and it's a dish that's good for anyone on a wheat-free diet. It captures the colours and sunshine so well, I can almost imagine I'm on the Florida Keys. Florida always dazzles me with its beautiful beaches and gleaming white sands. I love to watch the wild dolphins and candy-pink sunsets. The food is just as enchanting and seems to reflect its candy-coloured environment. There's great seafood in Florida, but it tends to be deep-fried and in a sandwich, and the portion sizes are vast! So I've recreated similar but healthier flavours at home.

This is my lighter take on a Florida favourite

Serves 2
Preparation time 15 minutes
Cooking time 5 minutes

4 large scallops, sliced through the middle
8 raw king or tiger prawns, shelled
1 large free-range egg
1 avocado, halved and stoned
½ small red onion
1 tomato
Juice 1 lime
1 small handful fresh coriander leaves
2–3 tbsp vegetable oil, for frying
Sea salt and freshly ground black pepper

For the spicy cornmeal
100g cornmeal or fine polenta
1 tsp ground cumin
1 tsp ground coriander
1 tsp smoked paprika
½ tsp cayenne pepper
½ tsp garlic salt
Large pinch dried oregano

To serve
4 taco shells or soft flour tortillas
¼ Iceberg lettuce or 1 Little Gem lettuce, shredded
2 tbsp soured cream
1 tsp chopped jalapeño chilli

Firstly, wash the seafood and pat dry. Mix together the spicy cornmeal ingredients in a shallow bowl and beat the egg in another shallow bowl. Set both aside.

To make a salsa, roughly chop the avocado, tomato and onion. Mix together with the lime juice, coriander and seasoning. Set aside.

Dip the scallops and prawns in the egg, then toss in the cornmeal mix. Heat the oil in a frying pan and fry the prawns for about 2 minutes each side until pink and firm. Remove to a paper towel. Fry the scallops likewise – for 1–2 minutes on each side. If they're large, you may like to slice them in half.

To serve, half-fill the taco shells with lettuce then divide the seafood between them, followed by the avocado salsa. Dollop with soured cream and sprinkle with the jalapeños. Alternatively, if using soft tortillas lay them flat and divide the seafood and salsa on top followed by the lettuce, cream and jalapeños. Roll up to eat.

27

Somerset cider and leek soup

I spent most of my teenage years in Somerset. At the time it seemed like the most boring place on earth (as *everything* does when you're a teenager), but now I appreciate and, dare I say, miss the beautiful greens and golden browns of the countryside.

One major draw for me was the local produce, something that I was always into. We would drive down little lanes and get homemade cider, free-range pork and knock-your-socks-off-strong cheddar cheese. Then it was back to the Aga for mulled cider, huge roasts and warming soups – all dishes that my mother excels at! This is a dish to challenge our French friends' classic onion soup, with leeks, cider and cheddar.

This is a dish to challenge our French friends' classic onion soup

Serves 4
Preparation time   15 minutes
Cooking time   1½ hours

50g butter or 3 tbsp olive oil
2 cloves garlic, crushed
3 large onions, thinly sliced
1 sprig thyme
250ml dry cider
1 litre chicken or vegetable stock (can be made with a cube or bouillon powder)
2 leeks, thinly sliced
4 tbsp grated mature Cheddar cheese
Sea salt and freshly ground black pepper

Heat the butter in a large heavy-based saucepan until it melts, then add the garlic and onion and fry gently. Cook the onions very slowly for about 30 minutes until they are really caramelised and golden brown. Then add the thyme.

Pour in the cider and stock, bring to the boil and simmer for 30 minutes. Add the leeks to the saucepan, check the seasoning and cook for a further 20 minutes.

To serve, preheat the grill. Divide the soup between four bowls, top with the cheese then pop under the hot grill for 2–3 minutes until melted and bubbling.

Sea bass on roasted fennel with Niçoise dressing

Cooking for events can be stressful. One evening I was cooking a dinner for thirty people, but my ingredients hadn't arrived. This was a last-minute dish I came up with, using only what I could find and buy in the shop nearby, and it went down very well. I figure if it's possible to cook up thirty portions with the clock ticking, then two at home should be easy!

This was a last-minute dish I came up with

Serves 2
Preparation time   15 minutes
Cooking time   25 minutes

1 bulb fennel
2 tbsp extra virgin olive oil, plus a little extra for cooking the fish
2 free-range eggs (or 4 quails' eggs, which are especially good for dinner parties)
175g French beans
½ tsp Dijon mustard
1 tbsp white wine vinegar
1 tbsp black Kalamata olives, stoned and sliced
4 cherry tomatoes, quartered
1 small red onion, finely diced
Small handful fresh basil
Squeeze lemon
2 fillets sea bass, about 125g each
Sea salt and freshly ground black pepper

Preheat the oven to 180°C, Gas Mark 4. Cut the fennel into quarters and place in a small baking dish. Drizzle with olive oil, season and pop in the oven for 20 minutes until just softened but still firm.

Meanwhile, place the eggs in a small saucepan, cover with cold water and bring to the boil. Simmer for 4 minutes then drain and run under cold water in a colander until cool, and peel. This will give you soft yolks, which the French call *oeufs mollet* – ooh la la! Set aside. If using quails' eggs cook them for 3 minutes and serve hard-boiled so they will be easier to peel.

Top-and-tail the beans and boil in lightly salted water for 3 minutes. Drain and cool, like the eggs, under cold running water to keep their bright green colour. Pat dry with a paper towel and cut into 3cm lengths.

To make the dressing, mash the eggs in a large mixing bowl with a fork, then add the mustard and vinegar, some seasoning and whisk in the olive oil. Toss in the olives, tomatoes and onion. Tear the basil into shreds and mix in also.

Heat up a large frying pan and add a splash of olive oil. Season the fish and lie the fillets skin-side down in the pan. Cook for around 5 minutes on this side, until really golden and crispy, then turn over and finish cooking for a further minute on the other side (you may need to cook for slightly longer depending on the thickness of the fish). Remove from the pan and squeeze a little lemon over the fillets.

To serve, place the fennel in the middle of the plate, then put the fish on top. Spoon the dressing over and around the fish.

STORE CUPBOARD
AND FREEZER SPECIALS

As much as I love shopping – and **believe me I really do**, be it clothes, make-up or food – sometimes I just don't have the time to keep my fridge stocked.

There are those moments when you want something homemade from whatever is hanging around in the cupboard or freezer that's still tasty and wholesome. So this section is all about **rustling up something fab last minute, without putting a hair out of place!** There are also some tips on pages 208–11 on how to shop for food in style and keep your cupboards, fridge and freezer well stocked with both fresh and non-perishable standbys.

Chestnut and porcini risotto

Risottos are fail-safe standby suppers. There seems to be a mystique surrounding the making of risotto but, when you have the hang of it, it's so simple! You need to give them a little bit of love and attention and work with them, that's all. Chestnuts and porcini mushrooms make this an especially warming and comforting risotto. Dried porcini mushrooms are great; they add an almost zero calorie meatiness to many dishes, from lasagne to soups. I have added less butter and cheese than in a normal risotto, too. The dish doesn't suffer in any way, but if you want to add a little bit more, feel free. I quite like eating a less fat-laden risotto, as you don't feel heavy afterwards and it's still a very satisfying meal.

Chestnuts and porcini mushrooms make this an especially warming and comforting risotto

Serves 2–3
Preparation time   5 minutes
Cooking time   30 minutes

50g dried porcini mushrooms
2–3 tbsp olive oil
1 onion, finely chopped
2 cloves garlic, crushed
200g risotto rice, such as Arborio or my favourite Vialone Nano
5 tbsp dry white wine
50g cooked vacuum-packed chestnuts
1 sprig rosemary
800ml–1litre warm vegetable stock (can be made with a cube or bouillon powder)
50g freshly grated Parmesan cheese
Small knob butter
Sea salt and freshly ground black pepper

Place the mushrooms into a small bowl and cover with a mug of boiling water. Heat a tablespoon of oil in a deep heavy-based frying pan or sauté dish. Gently fry the onion and garlic for about 5 minutes until translucent. Drain the mushrooms (reserving the water and using it to help make up the stock amount) and chop roughly. Add to the pan along with another tablespoon of oil. Stir in the rice and continue to cook for 5 minutes. Add the wine, stir until absorbed and then crumble in the chestnuts and add the rosemary.

Add the stock ladle by ladle, letting the liquid absorb after each addition. Give the risotto some tender loving care and continue cooking like this – it should take about 20 minutes. Do check as you go along, as rice can vary from type to type. You want it to be *al dente* – still firm to bite – and creamy. Also, season at this point. Finally, stir in the butter and most of the Parmesan, leave for two minutes then serve in shallow bowls, sprinkled with the last of the cheese.

Turn to page 103 for another recipe using chestnuts

Nasi Goreng

Bali has always been one of my favourite places. I first travelled there when I was eleven and it seemed like the true example of paradise, all white sandy beaches and green coconuts. Then there was the revelation of the food! The flavours bounce off the plate: sweet saté sauces, spicy chillies and desserts in luminous colours. It really opened my eyes and fuelled my foodie passion. Nasi Goreng is my best quick lunch or supper, you can use up all sorts of leftovers or just make it with vegetables. I always have the core ingredients at hand in my kitchen.

Nasi Goreng is my best quick lunch or supper

Serves 2
Preparation time   15 minutes
Cooking time   15 minutes

1 tbsp sesame oil
2 cloves garlic, crushed
4 spring onions, finely sliced
1 red chilli, slit, deseeded and sliced (or ½ tsp dried chilli flakes)
1–2 tsp curry powder
1 tbsp vegetable oil, plus extra for cooking the eggs
200g frozen prawns, thawed
200g cooked basmati rice, cooled (for my method see below. 75g raw rice will give you approx 200g when cooked)
1 tbsp sweet chilli sauce
1 tbsp soy sauce
2 free-range eggs
1 tbsp salted peanuts, chopped
1 lime, cut in wedges
Sea salt and freshly ground black pepper

Heat the sesame oil in a wok or frying pan and gently fry the garlic, spring onion and chilli with the curry powder (add to taste). Add a tablespoon of vegetable oil then toss in the prawns and cook for 3 minutes until browned. Stir in the cooked rice and reheat until piping hot. Stir in the sweet chilli sauce and soy sauce.

In a separate frying pan, fry both eggs off in a little more hot oil. To serve, divide the rice between two warmed plates and top with the softly fried eggs. Serve sprinkled with peanuts and lime wedges alongside.

How I cook rice

Allow 50g rice a head to serve as an accompaniment, less for a pilaf-style dish with other additions. Choose a good quality basmati rice for a better fragrance and texture.

Whenever I cook rice I always do lots extra, to use in dishes like this. You really need to have either leftover rice or rice that has just been cooked and cooled.

To cook the rice, measure it in a measuring jug or mug and tip it into a saucepan. Then add double that volume of water, bring to the boil, stir and cover. Simmer until all the water has been absorbed. Keep the saucepan covered while the rice is simmering. Remove from the heat, still covered, and allow to stand for 5 minutes. Fork through and use or cool for later.

NB – when reheating cooked rice, always ensure it is very hot when you serve it.

White bean and truffle soup

Meals made from store cupboard ingredients sound like they'll be boring and unhealthy. Not so! This is a velvety smooth, chic little soup that wouldn't look out of place on a restaurant menu. I'm a great believer in avoiding stress wherever possible and this is a good dinner party starter that will leave you plenty of time to beautify yourself or organise the kids/boyfriend/feed the cat, etc. It's actually very healthy too: all pulses and beans are low on the glycaemic index (they release sugar slowly into the bloodstream) so they keep you feeling full for longer, plus they last for ages dried or in tins in the cupboard.

This is a velvety smooth, chic little soup

Serves 4
Preparation time 5 minutes
Cooking time 30 minutes

25g butter
1 onion, finely diced
2 cloves garlic, crushed
2x400g cans white beans, such as cannellini or butter beans, drained
1 sprig thyme
400ml milk
600ml chicken or vegetable stock
A little truffle oil, to serve
Sea salt and freshly ground black pepper

Heat the butter gently in a large saucepan then sweat down the onion and garlic for about 5 minutes until translucent. Add the white beans, thyme, milk and stock and simmer for 20 minutes. Check the seasoning, remove the thyme and blitz the liquid in a food processor until very smooth. Strain through a sieve, pressing the mixture through with the back of a ladle. Pour into bowls and drizzle with truffle oil.

You can also top this soup with crispy Serrano ham or shavings of truffle pecorino.

Turn to page 91 for another recipe using truffle oil

Summer fruit and pear crumble

Crumbles are, quite frankly, most people's favourite puddings! I love them and find nothing more comforting than a bowl of golden, knobbly crumble, tangy fruit and creamy custard. It's also the quickest pud to make and can be knocked up with the most basic ingredients. Using summer fruits and pears makes it slightly different, and you can also experiment and use whatever you have at hand: apples, rhubarb, caramelised bananas, plums or peaches. The same applies to the flours and spices you use. Having more fruit than topping means it's not too heavy, it's healthier and you still get that intense fruity flavour.

A bowl of golden, knobbly crumble, tangy fruit and creamy custard

Serves 4
Preparation time   10 minutes
Cooking time   30 minutes

1 x 400g can pear quarters in
natural juice, drained
300g frozen summer fruits
3 tbsp caster sugar, or 2 tbsp fruit sugar
1 tbsp cassis (optional)

For the topping
125g plain flour (substitute 75g with spelt or
wholemeal flour for a healthier option)
60g butter
Pinch of salt
25g light brown sugar

Preheat the oven to 170°C, Gas Mark 3. Place the two fruits, sugar and cassis, if using, into a saucepan and bring to the boil. Remove from the heat and pour into a medium baking dish.

Take a large mixing bowl and combine the flour, butter and salt. Then rub the mixture together to form a crumb-like consistency and mix in the light brown sugar. Sprinkle over the top of the fruit mix and bake for 30 minutes or until golden on top. Serve with vanilla ice cream or custard.

Grilled polenta with red pepper and anchovy salad

This colourful and flavoursome dish can be made just from a well-stocked cupboard. So it really is a miracle meal! The salty anchovies work so well with the sweet red peppers and canary-yellow polenta wedges. It's also a low-fat dish, so ideal for a quick, healthy supper.

The salty anchovies work so well with the sweet red peppers

Serves 4
Preparation time 20 minutes, plus chilling time
Cooking time 20 minutes

400ml vegetable stock (can be made with a cube)
200g polenta
Pinch dried thyme
Pinch dried oregano
Pinch dried rosemary
50g freshly grated Parmesan cheese
Olive oil, plus 2 tsp for dressing
100g chargrilled peppers, available from delis and supermarkets in jars
50g can anchovies
Sea salt and freshly ground black pepper

For the dressing
2 tbsp stoned black olives, finely chopped
1 tbsp white balsamic vinegar
1 garlic clove, crushed
Small handful basil leaves

Bring the stock to the boil in a large non-stick saucepan and pour in the polenta in a steady stream, stirring briskly as you pour. Continue stirring until the polenta becomes thick then turn down the heat to a gentle simmer and cook according to pack instructions, usually for about 5–8 minutes. Take care as it will spit – you might want to partially cover the pan with the lid.

Remove the saucepan from the heat and mix in the herbs, Parmesan and 1 tbsp of oil. Check the seasoning. Line a shallow tin with clingfilm and pour in the polenta mix. Spread and smooth the mixture until it's about 1cm deep. Leave it to cool and set. Chill in the fridge until required.

Drain the peppers from the oil or brine they're preserved in and cut into thick strips. Mix all the dressing ingredients together with a little seasoning and use this to dress the peppers. Drain the anchovies, pat dry and cut into thin slivers.

Remove the polenta from the fridge and cut into wedges. Heat a griddle pan until very hot, and chargrill the wedges for about 5 minutes on each side, until black griddle lines appear. Serve with the salad and top with slivers of anchovy.

EASY PACKED LUNCHES

People tend to think packed lunches are slightly un-glam.
I had one friend who took them to the next level and would bring a little
tub of caviar, some blinis, a tin of foie gras pâté and a mini bottle of
champers on a plane with him as he hated airline food, but I don't think it
would go down so well with your boss if you turned up with a lunch like
that at work, even if you do have that kind of cash to splash!

The words 'packed lunch' tend to evoke images of soggy sandwiches made
with cardboard-like white sliced bread and the odd packet of undesirable
crisps. If you want to keep your figure looking good while still being able
to enjoy your food it's **a great idea to make your own**. Apart from
anything else, the awful offerings you can buy in shops are often tasteless,
of a rather dubious freshness and packed full of nasties like preservatives
and additives. Here are **my yummy packed lunch alternatives . . .**

Lamb and Greek salad pittas

This is like an upmarket Greek gyros (or kebab). I have a naughty tendency to consume gyros in the late afternoons in Greece. The combination of the salty sea air and the smell of aromatic meats makes for an incredibly tasty, hand-held dish, and it keeps me going until our balmy late-night suppers under the grapevines. Gyros are not good for the waistline though, so my version is made with good meat that has less fat and more salad. It's a blindingly good packed lunch, but your colleagues will get jealous . . . maybe make a few extra, or just recommend they buy their own copy of *Fabulous Food*!

A blindingly good packed lunch, but your colleagues will get jealous . . .

Serves 2
Preparation time   15 minutes
Cooking time   10 minutes

1 tbsp olive oil
2 lamb leg steaks, about 100g each, fat trimmed off
2 wholemeal pittas, warmed and split open
1 tomato, sliced
½ red onion, sliced
100g feta cheese, ideally reduced fat, crumbled
Pinch of oregano
Sea salt and freshly ground black pepper

For the tzatziki
100ml 0% fat Greek yogurt
¼ cucumber
1 clove garlic, crushed

To make the tzatziki, grate the cucumber coarsely, place in a colander and press out any excess water. Tip the cucumber into a bowl and mix with the yogurt and seasoning.

Heat the oil in a frying pan and cook the lamb for 3–5 minutes on each side until just firm but still tender, it should be slightly pink in the middle. Allow to cool. To assemble, slice the lamb thinly and layer into a split pitta with the tomato, onion and crumbled feta and pinches of oregano. Top with dollops of tzatziki and serve.

Turn to pages 73, 102 and 143 for more recipes using feta

Courgette, onion and green olive frittatas

This is an excellent quick high-protein lunch or snack. Frittatas are about as simple as it gets and bursting full of flavour. They also taste better when served cold, so they are the perfect packed lunch option. Frittatas are basically omelettes, and you can experiment with lots of different flavours. I sometimes line the muffin tins with smoked salmon or bacon and fill them with chive-laced eggs or even blue cheese and roasted vegetables. The choices are endless . . .

Frittatas are about as simple as it gets and bursting full of flavour

Makes 6
Preparation time   15 minutes
Cooking time   30 minutes

1–2 tbsp olive oil, plus extra to grease muffin tins
1 clove garlic, finely chopped
1 red onion, diced
1 courgette, diced
1 tbsp stoned green olives, sliced into rings
1 sprig basil, chopped
50g rindless goats' cheese, crumbled
4 eggs
2 tbsp milk
Sea salt and freshly ground black pepper

Preheat the oven to 200°C, Gas Mark 6. Grease a deep 6-hole muffin tin with oil.

Fry the garlic, onion and courgette in a little olive oil for about 7 minutes until soft. Scatter between the muffin moulds. Divide the olives, basil and goats' cheese between each muffin and add on top.

Whisk the eggs with the milk, salt and pepper. Pour the egg mix into each mould and stir gently to mix. Bake for 15–20 minutes until lightly firm on top, remove from the oven and leave to cool for 5 minutes. Turn out, cool and serve.

Roast squash, Dolcelatte and rocket wraps

Vegetarians sometimes get a raw deal, and even I am guilty of overlooking their needs now and again (it's pure laziness on the chef's part: meat is so simple and so tasty!). I was brought up a veggie for a while though, and I do think for some people it's a good way of eating.

This wrap is really tasty. The sweetness of the squash and the salty creaminess of the cheese work so well together that I would eat this any day. (If you are a meat lover, it works well with a few slivers of Parma ham too.)

The sweetness of the squash and the salty creaminess of the cheese work so well together

Makes 2
Preparation time   15 minutes
Cooking time   30 minutes

½ butternut squash
Olive oil, to drizzle
Maple syrup, to drizzle (optional)
Pinch dried chilli flakes or powder
2 seeded wraps (or plain)
1–2 tbsp walnuts, chopped
50g Dolcelatte (or Dolce Blue) cheese, crumbled
Small handful of rocket
Sea salt and freshly ground black pepper

Preheat the oven to 200 °C, Gas Mark 6. Peel, deseed and then cut the squash into small cubes. Lay the cubes on a tray, season and drizzle with oil and maple syrup (optional) then sprinkle with the chilli. Roast for 30 minutes until softened, stirring once or twice, then remove and allow to cool.

Take the two wraps and lay them on a chopping board. Scatter over the squash, cheese and walnuts. Top with a sprinkling of rocket and roll up firmly. Then, cut in half and wrap in foil or clingfilm. Your lovely veggie wrap lunch is now ready!

Poached salmon and ravigote potatoes

Classic flavours are always the best, and poached salmon with a beautiful potato salad has got to be one of the top classic dishes to serve cold. From a health point of view, the salmon contains some Omega-3 oils and if you add a handful of rocket you have iron. This is a hearty lunch that will keep you going till supper. It also makes a *très* chic starter when served in mini portions.

This is a hearty lunch that will keep you going till supper

Serves 2
Preparation time 12 minutes,
plus cooling time
Cooking time 20 minutes

400g new potatoes
2 fillets fresh salmon, about 125g each
Juice 1 lemon
1 tbsp balsamic vinegar
1 tbsp olive oil
1 tbsp chopped tarragon
1 tbsp chopped flat-leaf parsley
1–2 tbsp capers, chopped if large
1 small shallot, finely chopped
A little rocket, to serve
Sea salt and freshly ground black pepper

Boil the potatoes in lightly salted water for 15–20 minutes until tender. Drain and cool until you can comfortably handle them.

While the potatoes cool, poach the salmon. Place the slices in a deep frying pan and cover with water. Squeeze in the lemon and add salt and pepper. Bring gently up to the boil, then take off the heat and leave for 10 minutes until the flesh feels just firm when pressed. Drain and allow to cool.

Break up the warm potatoes with your hands. Add the vinegar and olive oil and mix well, then add in the herbs, capers and shallot. You want the flavours to infuse the potatoes while they are still warm. Season and leave to cool.

When you are ready to go out, just pop the salmon and potatoes in a container, add some rocket salad and enjoy! Don't forget to pack some forks.

 Turn to page 54 to use any leftover flat-leaf parsley

Chicken, ginger and hoisin lettuce wraps

I travel a lot and rarely find anything satisfying to eat; it's very hard to find fresh, healthy food on the road and everything is made of wheat. Wheat is about the worst ingredient to eat when travelling as it makes people feel so bloated. This is a nifty little packed lunch inspired by a Chinese dish I love (only, the original uses minced pigeon meat!). You can wrap these up and eat by hand wherever you are. The ginger is great for combating travel sickness and the flavours are fresh and pure, something that I long for from food on the go . . .

This is a nifty little packed lunch inspired by a Chinese dish I love

Makes 16 to serve 4
Preparation time   15 minutes
Cooking time   10 minutes

1 tbsp sesame oil
2 skinless, boneless organic chicken breasts, cut in thin strips
1 red pepper, cored and sliced in thin strips
2 spring onions, trimmed and cut in thin sticks
1 x 200g can bamboo shoots, drained and cut in thin sticks
1 carrot, cut in thin sticks
2cm piece fresh root ginger, peeled and grated
2 tsp hoisin sauce
2 tsp oyster sauce
Big pinch sesame seeds (optional)
About 16 outer leaves of Little Gem lettuce (or 8 Iceberg leaves, split in half), to serve.

Heat a wok or large frying pan and add the sesame oil. Stir-fry the chicken strips for 2 minutes and then add the vegetables and ginger.

Cook for a further 5–7 minutes, until the vegetables are cooked but still crisp. Mix in both sauces, cook for a further minute. Check the seasoning and finally add the sesame seeds, if you have them.

Leave to cool. Trim the stems of the lettuce leaves so they will roll easily, then spoon in the filling and roll up, securing each one with a wooden cocktail stick. Allow 4 rolls per serving.

Turn to pages 82, 96, 109, 189 and 206 for more recipes using fresh root ginger

Guilt-free comfort food

SAVOURY COMFORT FOOD WITHOUT THE GUILT

There are two types of people in this world – those who eat more when feeling down and those who stop eating when feeling down. I, quite frankly, chow down when depressed . . . I barely come up for air.
I have always been rather jealous of the non-eating types as at least they come out of the gloom with a new size-ten physique, whereas I come out with an extra chin!

Saying that, **when you're feeling low you need especially good nutrition** as your immune system takes a dive when you're upset. A size-ten bottom is all well and good, but paired with a runny nose and sneezing it's not so hot.

Let's face it, our climate is more Russia than Riviera, so sometimes only a pile of fluffy mash and some rich stew will do. This section is about how to get that **comfort factor** without doing too much damage.

Beef stifado

Greek cuisine includes lots of stews and casseroles. You'd think that stews don't exactly go with the searing hot sunshine there, but the smells of cinnamon-laced beef and rabbit stifado with homemade olive oil and oregano chips wafting down the beach gets me every time. Beef stifado is something different from the usual British stews, and the cinnamon and orange give this dish a real warmth. This dish also works with any other meat, such as chicken, lamb or, the classic, rabbit.

The cinnamon and orange give this dish a real warmth

Serves 4
Preparation time   15 minutes
Cooking time   80 minutes

800g lean beef braising steak
5 tbsp olive oil
10 baby onions, peeled
1 tsp ground cinnamon
1 small whole bulb garlic, peeled (see below for my method of peeling garlic the easy way)
250ml red wine
2 400g cans chopped tomatoes
1 bay leaf
1 small orange: large strip of zest and all the juice
500–600g new potatoes
1 tsp dried oregano
Leaves from a small bunch flat-leaf parsley, roughly chopped
Sea salt and freshly ground black pepper

Cube the beef into fairly large chunks, about 2cm big. Heat up a large frying pan, add 1 tbsp of oil and fry the beef on a high heat to brown. In a separate large heavy-based saucepan add another 2 tbsp of oil and brown the onions, cinnamon and all but two of the garlic cloves. Then add the browned beef and the wine. Bring to the boil then simmer uncovered for about 15 minutes, until reduced down by half.

Add the tomatoes, bay leaf, orange zest and juice. Return to the boil and simmer while covered for about 1–1¼ hours or until the meat is tender, then remove from the heat.

Meanwhile, cut the potatoes into roughly even-sized chunks. Parboil in plenty of boiling water for 10 minutes then drain well. Heat the remaining oil in the same pan. Toss the potatoes back in, cooking until nicely browned. Crush the reserved garlic and add to the potatoes with seasoning and oregano. Cook for another 10 minutes until tender. Serve with the beef stifado, and sprinkle with the parsley.

How to peel garlic cloves easily
Place each garlic clove one by one on a chopping board. Put the blade of a large knife on top, flat-side down and bang hard with your fist on the flat blade. This will partially crush the cloves and make them easy to peel.

Neeps- and tatties-topped cottage pie

When clients of mine used to ask for dishes like cottage pie, I would think, How boring! Why employ a private chef for simple things like that? The reason is you can't beat homemade comfort food! That's why no one can match your mother's cooking and why we are all comforted by the old favourites. My version ups the vegetable content, lowers the fat and cuts out thickeners like flour, so it's better for you but still essentially tastes of what it should: rich meaty beef and creamy mash.

We are all comforted by the old favourites

Serves 4
Preparation time   10 minutes
Cooking time   1¼ hours

500g good quality lean steak
2 sticks celery
2 carrots
1 onion
2 cloves garlic
1 tbsp olive oil
2 bay leaves
50ml whisky (optional)
500ml of stock (can be either vegetable, beef or chicken)
1 tbsp tomato purée
2 tbsp Worcestershire sauce
1 small swede, about 500g
1 medium potato, about 350g
2 tbsp milk
25g butter
100g frozen peas
20g mature Cheddar, grated

Firstly, cut the beef into cubes and blitz in a blender until it has a mince-like texture. Finely chop the onion, celery and carrot and crush the garlic. Then heat up a saucepan and sweat the vegetables off in the little olive oil.

Heat a separate frying pan until very hot. Without using any oil, fry the beef off in batches, getting as much colour as possible and also breaking up any big chunks as you go along. This is also a good time to season the meat. Add the beef to the saucepan with the vegetables and mix well. Pour in the whisky, bay leaves and stock. Then add the Worcestershire sauce and tomato purée. Bring to the boil, season then turn down and simmer for 30 minutes. Remove the bay leaves.

Preheat the oven to 200°C, Gas Mark 5. Peel and cube the potato and swede and place in a saucepan. Cover with water, bring to the boil and add salt. Simmer for 20 minutes or until cooked throughout. Drain off. Add the milk, butter, salt and pepper and roughly mash.

Add the peas to the beef, continue cooking for 5 minutes and check the seasoning. Pour the beef mix into a baking dish and spread the potato mix on top. Sprinkle over the cheese and bake for 20 minutes or until golden brown and bubbling

 Turn to page 53 to use any leftover celery and carrots

Thyme and cider pot-roasted chicken

If I want to feel instant comfort at home, I cook a chicken – be it roasted or braised. A chicken will fill your home with the most wonderful smells, and fill your belly with nutritious and wonderful food.

My mother cooks a fantastic roast chicken and it's this simple dish that I crave more than anything. I love my Le Creuset pans, which are just the same as the pans that my mother used; it's a perfect tradition. Again using the wonderful cider we had in Somerset, I semi-braise this chicken with all of nature's wonderful aromatics. This is comfort food extraordinaire!

This is comfort food extraordinaire!

Serves 4
Preparation time   15 minutes
Cooking time   2 hours

1 small–medium free-range chicken, about
1.5kg
2 tbsp olive oil
25g butter
2 carrots, cut in small neat pieces
2 medium leeks, trimmed and sliced
1 stick celery, trimmed and sliced
1 onion, roughly chopped
4 sprigs thyme
2 cloves garlic, chopped
2 bay leaves
300ml dry cider
500ml chicken stock
A little chopped fresh parsley
Sea salt & freshly ground black pepper

Untruss the bird (i.e. untie the legs) and pull out the pad of fat from inside the cavity. Trim off any fatty skin. In a medium-size flameproof or cast-iron casserole dish, heat the oil and brown the bird, pressing down on the breast side. Remove to a plate.

Add the butter to the dish and toss in the prepared vegetables, stirring to coat in the fat. Mix in the garlic, thyme and bay. Heat until sizzling, then cover and cook on a medium heat for about 5 minutes until softened.

Nestle the chicken in the vegetables. Pour in the cider and bring to the boil. Lower to a simmer and allow to bubble for about 3 minutes then pour in the stock and return to the boil. Season, cover and cook on a very gentle heat for 1½ to 2 hours until the legs of the chicken are tender.

Remove the bird to a chopping board and stand for 10 minutes to let the flesh rest (don't worry, it won't lose heat). Continue to cook the pan juices until reduced by half. Scoop the vegetables out on to a warm serving platter with a slotted spoon. Cut the bird into pieces as you like, into neatly carved slices or just rustic chunks. Place on top of the vegetables, strain over the pan juices and scatter with some parsley to serve.

Duck and sour cherry ragu with buttered noodles

Duck is a fantastically flavoursome meat. It's often thought of as being high in fat, but if you remove the skin it's a great meat. Even duck can be ruined, though. I recently bought a readymade meal — *purely* in the name of research, I swear! The duck was a miserable piece of grey meat, with no trace of its potential glory – the whole ensemble was a major let-down. In fact I even woke up the next morning with a junk-food hangover. Never again!

My ragu captures the true taste of duck and adds even more flavour with the livers, and with the cherries for a touch of sweetness.

Duck is a fantastically flavoursome meat

Serves 2
Preparation time   20 minutes
Cooking time   40 minutes

1 onion, finely chopped
1 clove garlic, crushed
2 tbsp olive oil
2 skinless, boneless duck breasts,
about 125g each
100g duck or chicken liver (organic if possible)
Leaves of 1 sprig thyme
1 tbsp dried sour cherries (or dried cranberries)
1 tsp orange zest
100ml red wine
100ml port
200ml chicken stock
2 juniper berries, crushed roughly
1 bay leaf
1 tsp tomato purée
1 tbsp cornflour
100g buckwheat noodles (or use pasta noodles,
like tagliatelle)
Small knob of butter
Small handful flat-leaf parsley
Sea salt and freshly ground black pepper

Finely chop the onion and garlic and then sweat off in a little oil for about 5 minutes until softened. Remove and cool.

Blitz the duck breasts and livers in a blender or food processor using the pulse button, until they resemble a coarse mince. Tip into a bowl and mix with the onion and garlic, along with the thyme, cherries and orange zest.

Heat a little oil in a deep frying pan and brown the meat for 10 minutes or until golden brown. Then add the wine and port and simmer for 5 minutes, then add the stock, juniper berries, bay leaf and tomato purée.

Bring the meat mix to the boil, and then season and simmer for 20 minutes. Whisk the cornflour with a little cold water and beat it into the sauce to thicken it.

Boil the noodles according to the packet instructions. Then drain, season, toss in the butter and mix with the meat. Serve with a sprinkling of chopped parsley.

Honey- and lavender-glazed lamb with potato gratin

Honey and lavender sounds like a very girly and whimsical set of flavours, but when combined with the other herbs the flavours blend together smoothly. A leg of lamb for Sunday lunch is heavenly and this recipe is a change from the usual rosemary and lemon that I use. This recipe was inspired by the south of France, where they use beautiful aromatic herbs in everything from sweets to roasted vegetables, and of course they love their gratin. I had a cook-off with Jean Christophe Novelli recently where I cooked a fantastic healthy version of the traditionally naughty potato dish. They both tasted extremely good but I like to think I proved that it's possible to make comforting classics without an assault on the waistline!

This recipe was inspired by the south of France

Serves 4
Preparation time   15 minutes
Cooking time   1½ hours

1 1.5 kg leg of lamb, boned, trimmed of excess fat and rolled (rolled means tied into shape for easy cooking and neat carving!)
3–4 tbsp olive oil
6 potatoes, about 1kg in total, peeled
2 onions, ideally red, sliced thinly
20g butter, unsalted
250ml lamb or vegetable stock
2 tbsp clear honey
2 heads lavender, petals picked
3 cloves garlic, sliced
2 sprigs thyme, roughly chopped
Leaves from 2 sprigs rosemary, roughly chopped
Sea salt and freshly ground black pepper

Preheat the oven to 200°C, Gas Mark 6. Heat a large frying pan until very hot. Season the lamb and add a tablespoon olive oil to the pan. Press the lamb into the hot pan, turning to brown on all sides. You may need a thick clean tea towel to help with this! Then remove and put on to one side.

Take a deep baking dish and grease with a little more olive oil. Slice the potatoes finely and layer in the dish with the onions. Dot with butter and season as you layer. Pour over the stock and place in the oven for 20 minutes.

Take the gratin out of the oven and lay the lamb on top of the potatoes. Return and cook for 30 minutes. Remove again and drizzle with the honey; sprinkle with the lavender and tuck the garlic and other herbs around. Return to the oven for about another 30 minutes until the lamb is cooked through (it should be very slightly pink inside). Remove from the oven and stand for 10 minutes before slicing and serving. Delicious served with French beans and carrots.

Butternut squash and almond risotto

This may seem like a strange combination of flavours, but I first tasted it in northern Italy years ago, by one of the lakes. Then I had it in the form of squash and almond ravioli, but it works well as a risotto. The sweetness of the squash and ameretti is a fragrant and interesting taste, quite gentle and soothing. If you want to add a little more of a savoury aspect, add some roughly chopped sage leaves. This is also a great dish for vegetarians.

A great dish for vegetarians

Serves 2
Preparation time   15 minutes
Cooking time   50 minutes

½ small butternut squash, about 350g
2 tbsp olive oil
1 onion, finely diced
2 cloves garlic, crushed
200g risotto rice, such as Arborio or Vialone Nano, my favourite
75ml white wine
800ml vegetable stock, warmed
1–2 tbsp amaretto liqueur
Small knob butter
25g freshly grated Parmesan
2 tbsp whole blanched and toasted almonds, roughly chopped
2 amaretti biscuits, crumbled
Sea salt and freshly ground black pepper

Preheat the oven to 200°C, Gas Mark 6. Peel, deseed and dice the squash into 1cm cubes. Place in a single layer on a non-stick baking tray and roast for 20 minutes. Then remove and leave to cool.

Heat a tablespoon of oil in a deep heavy-based frying or sauté pan. Add the onion and garlic and fry gently for 5 minutes until softened and translucent. Add another tablespoon of oil, heat for a few seconds then stir in the rice, coating the grains in oil and continue cooking for 1–2 minutes. Pour in the wine and stir until it is all absorbed.

Then, using a ladle, gradually add the stock. Stir the grains after each ladleful and wait until the liquid is absorbed before adding more. After 10 minutes or so, mix in the squash. After 15 minutes mix in the amaretto to taste and cook for a further minute or so. By this time the grains should be *al dente* and the mixture nice and creamy.

Finally, stir in the butter, Parmesan and almonds. Check the seasoning and divide between two plates or shallow bowls. Crumble over the amaretti just before serving.

Thai sweetcorn and sweet potato chowder

This is a dish I invented recently in my kitchen. Dishes are often born of necessity, as this one was with only a strange selection of ingredients to hand. I fancied a soup, but something substantial, creamy and with a little spice. I happened to have some leftover aromatics from a curry, a can of low-fat coconut milk, some sweetcorn and an old sweet potato. *Et voilà!* Lightly spiced chowder that doesn't leave your arteries feeling clogged, yet has that comfort factor. It's very quick to make, too. You can add seafood to it if you like, in keeping with classic chowder recipes – experiment a little!

Something substantial, creamy and with a little spice

Serves 4
Preparation time   15 minutes
Cooking time   30 minutes

1 onion, finely chopped
1 garlic clove, crushed
3cm piece fresh root ginger, grated
1 red chilli, slit, deseeded and chopped
2 tbsp vegetable oil
1 tsp Thai curry paste
1 small sweet potato, peeled and finely chopped
400ml can half-fat coconut milk
300ml vegetable stock
½ 198g can sweetcorn, drained
Small handful fresh coriander
Juice 1 lime, to serve
Sea salt and freshly ground black pepper

Gently fry the onion, garlic, ginger and chilli in the oil for 5–7 minutes until translucent then add the Thai curry paste and stir well.

Add the sweet potato along with the coconut milk and stock. Season and bring to the boil, then lower the heat and simmer for 20 minutes. Add the sweetcorn and reheat. I like the sweet potato in this soup just semi-crushed so I blitz it with a handheld blender, but you could mash the sweet potato on the pan sides with a fork instead.

Check the seasoning and add coriander and lime juice to taste. Serve piping hot in soup bowls.

 Turn to pages 19, 168-9 and 179 for more recipes using sweet potato

Calves' liver with caramelised shallots, Gorgonzola and roasted artichokes

This is an autumnal dish which is quick to make but still has a complexity of flavours. From a health point of view, I like replacing refined carbohydrates with vegetables, which is where the artichokes come in. Jerusalem artichokes have a fantastic nutty flavour and velvety texture when used in soups. Calves' liver is the refined liver of choice and has the benefit of being a good source of iron and vitamin B12.

An autumnal dish which is quick to make but still has a complexity of flavours

Serves 2
Preparation time 15 minutes
Cooking time 45 minutes

50g butter
8–10 shallots, or baby onions, sliced
2 sprigs thyme
1 tsp brown sugar
2 tbsp balsamic vinegar
1 tbsp port
200g Jerusalem artichokes, peeled and cut into medium chunks
Olive oil, to drizzle
50g Gorgonzola cheese
2 escalopes (thin slices) calves' liver, about 80g each
100g watercress
1 lemon
Sea salt and freshly ground black pepper

Preheat the oven to 200 °C, Gas Mark 6. Heat the butter in a frying pan and fry the shallots with the thyme until they start to brown. Stir in the sugar and continue cooking to caramelise them a little. Pour in the balsamic vinegar and port, and cook for about 10 minutes until reduced down and syrupy. Set aside.

Meanwhile, place the artichokes on a small baking tray, drizzle with some olive oil and season with salt and pepper. Roast in the oven for about 30 minutes until tender and golden. Remove from the oven and crumble the Gorgonzola cheese over the artichokes, then return to the oven and heat for a few minutes until melted. Keep the artichokes warm while you cook the liver.

Season the liver. Heat a frying pan until very hot, then add a tablespoon more oil and cook the escalopes for about 2–3 minutes on each side so they are still a little pink inside. When cooked, add the caramelised onions. Serve the liver with the artichokes and some watercress, dressed with the lemon juice.

Turn to page 200 for another recipe using Gorgonzola

Sardinian lamb stew with polenta chips

I spent one fantastic summer working around Europe. I ate the most wonderful and memorable meal in Sardinia. It was typical Italian generosity, with plate after plate of tantalising food. Dishes like Bottarga (dried mullets' roe) with celery leaves, braised artichoke stems, spicy salads and sweet Sardinian lobsters, all rounded off with Myrtle (a local liqueur) and orange-scented almond pastries. The flavours were robust and well-constructed. A meal that can only come from fresh good-quality produce. This is my version of their lamb stew, which I have served with polenta chips. Don't be afraid of olive oil, it's good for you and, after all, I believe in health before skinniness!

Serves 4
Preparation time   15 minutes
Cooking time   1½ hours

1 red onion, cut in chunks
2 carrots, sliced
2 tbsp olive oil, plus extra for frying the polenta
2 cloves garlic, crushed
600g lamb leg, fat trimmed off, cubed (or try the cheaper cut, neck fillet)
2 bulbs fennel, quartered and sliced
200ml white wine
400g can chopped tomatoes
½ tsp saffron strands
200ml lamb or vegetable stock (can be made with a cube or bouillon powder)
Small handful of flat-leaf parsley
Sea salt and freshly ground black pepper

For the polenta chips
150g polenta
40g sun-dried tomatoes, finely chopped
40g stoned black olives, finely chopped
75g freshly grated Parmesan

To make the polenta chips, put the polenta and 750ml of water into a pan and bring to the boil, stirring well. Add the sun-dried tomatoes and black olives and continue cooking for a further 15 minutes. (You may find the polenta spits a little so it's a good idea to half-cover the pan.) Add the Parmesan, a tablespoon of olive oil and check the seasoning. It may not need much salt because of the flavour of the cheese, tomatoes and olives. Line a shallow baking tray with clingfilm and pour in the polenta mix. Spread until level then allow to cool and chill until firm. Ideally the mix should be about 1½cm deep when spread out in the tray.

To make the stew, heat a large heavy-based saucepan and start to sweat off the onion and garlic in olive oil. Cook for about 5 minutes until translucent and then add the carrots and fennel. Continue to cook on a low heat for another 10 minutes.

Heat another tablespoon of oil in a large frying pan. Season and then seal the lamb until nicely brown and caramelised: this will give it lots of flavour. Add the lamb to the vegetable pan but keep the empty pan nearby. Pour the wine into this frying pan, scraping up the sediments. Allow it to bubble and cook down until reduced by half. Mix into the lamb and vegetables.

Add the tomatoes, saffron and stock. Bring to the boil, cover and simmer for 1 hour or until tender. Check the seasoning then add the parsley to the pan. While the lamb is cooking, cut the polenta into chunky chip-sized sticks. Heat up a frying pan, add a little olive oil to cover the base then gently fry the sticks until golden. You may have to do these in batches so you don't overload your pan. Remove the cooked sticks to a baking tray to keep warm in a low oven. Serve the chips with the delicious lamb stew.

Melanzane parmigiana

This Italian classic is seen on many menus, but can be a disappointment when served. I recently cooked for Italian friends (very risky, they can be tricky customers) in sunny St Tropez. Their faces sank when they saw I was cooking Melanzane Parmigiana. But in the end they loved the way I made it and the whole lot was polished off extremely quickly. It can be a wonderfully moreish dish, just make sure the aubergines are cooked before and don't let them soak up too much oil. It's also a quick dish to serve to vegetarians and carnivores alike.

A wonderfully moreish dish

Serves 4
Preparation time   15 minutes
Cooking time   40 minutes

About 4 tbsp olive oil
1 onion, chopped
3 cloves garlic, chopped
Pinch dried chilli flakes
1 x 400g can tomatoes
100ml dry white wine
1 bay leaf
Small bunch of basil, roughly chopped or torn
3 aubergines, sliced in 1cm rounds
2 150g balls of half-fat mozzarella, thinly sliced
100g freshly grated Parmesan cheese
Sea salt and freshly ground black pepper

Preheat the oven to 190°C, Gas Mark 5. Heat 1 tablespoon of oil in a medium saucepan and fry the onions and garlic for about 7 minutes until translucent.

Add the chilli, tomatoes, wine and bay leaf. Season, bring to the boil, then turn down to a simmer for 15 minutes until a rich tomato-sauce consistency has been achieved. Stir the basil into the sauce and remove from the heat.

Meanwhile, heat a griddle pan until very hot. Chargrill the aubergines on each side until tender and marked with dark grill lines.

Cover a medium-size dish with a layer of aubergine. Spoon over a third of the sauce, then a mixture of the two cheeses. Repeat twice more, making sure you finish with the cheese. Bake for 30 minutes until golden brown and bubbling. This is brilliant served with crusty bread and salad.

I'm not going to kid you about this; sugar is not and never will be good for your body. Too much can cause massive highs of energy (followed by massive lows) and it plays havoc with your weight. Plus, it can lead to far more serious problems, like diabetes. I know I'm starting to sound boring but I know everyone loves sweet treats now and again so **I've found ways around the sugar problem**.

If you are going to do something naughty, it might as well be really naughty. Go for a super-rich, dark, tall man . . .whoops! I mean a super-rich, dark chocolate – it will satisfy you more. Actually, it does kind of apply to men too: have a piece of low-fat (i.e. charmless, bad looking) supermarket pap and you will be left feeling deprived and end up eating (i.e. sleeping with) more than you intended to in the first place anyway.

This section is about minimising the damage at those times when only something gooey and sweet will do. I have thought through each recipe with looks and flavour in mind, cutting out as much unnecessary fat or sugar so that the important things take priority. At the end of the day, **if a girl needs chocolate I'm not going to stand in her way!**

Greek yogurt pannacottas with rhubarb compote

Little creamy wobbling jellies with deep-pink rhubarb and green pistachios: this comforting food just makes you want to smile. I love traditional pannacottas, but unfortunately they are usually made with double cream, sugar and rum, and although sometimes it feels like happiness can be found at the bottom of a cream pie, it doesn't help.

My pannacottas are made with wonderful Greek yogurt and natural honey, and so are better for you (the yogurt and honey both contain healthy bacteria) but still taste delicious. Don't be put off by the setting time: a little pre-planning goes a long way and, after all, anticipation is part of the joy of eating!

This comforting food just makes you want to smile

Serves 4
Preparation time 15 minutes, plus cooling and setting
for up to 5 hours
Cooking time 10 minutes

4 sheets leaf gelatine
200ml milk
1 vanilla pod
2 tbsp runny honey
250g tub 0% fat Greek yogurt

For the compote
200g pink rhubarb
75g fruit sugar, such as Fruisana,
or 100g caster sugar
1 tbsp chopped pistachios

First, to make the pannacottas, put the gelatine into a bowl and cover with cold water, then leave to one side until it becomes floppy.

Pour the milk into a saucepan and heat gently. Slit the vanilla pod on one side and open it up. Using the tip of a sharp knife, scrape out the sticky seeds and add to the milk with the empty pod and the honey. Bring gently to the boil and remove from the heat when it starts to bubble around the pan sides.

Drain off the gelatine sheets, squeezing out any excess water and stir into the hot milk until dissolved. Then beat in the yogurt until smooth and pour through a sieve into a bowl.

You can pour the mix into moulds now, but the vanilla seeds will sink to the bottom. So I prefer allowing the mixture to cool then chilling it in the fridge, stirring every 30 minutes or so, until it begins to set around the edges. As the mixture thickens you can then decant it into 4 lightly oiled, round metal moulds (of about 125ml capacity) or ramekins. Then chill for about 3 hours until completely set.

While the pannacottas are chilling, make the compote. Trim the rhubarb and cut into 3cm lengths. Heat the sugar with 100ml of water in a medium saucepan, stirring until dissolved. Add the rhubarb and bring to the boil. Simmer very gently for about 5 minutes, trying to keep the rhubarb pieces intact if possible. Remove and leave to cool.

When the compote is cooled, run a table knife around the pannacottas, shake out on to small dessert plates and serve the compote alongside. Sprinkle with the pistachios and serve.

Macadamia nut and lemon biscotti

I first discovered macadamia nuts in Australia. These rich, buttery nuts please me every time with their texture. Biscotti are dry Italian biscuits that only contain fat from nuts and egg yolks. They are perfect for dunking in coffee or sweet wines, are simple to make but very impressive. I also serve them with other puddings like the nectarine sabayon on page 68 or even the pannacottas on page 64. You can experiment with different flavours too, such as pistachio, pine nut and almond.

Simple to make but very impressive

Makes about 25 biscuits
Preparation time   15 minutes
Cooking time   30 minutes

200g macadamia nuts
250g plain flour
100g caster sugar (or try 75g fruit sugar, such as Fruisana)
1 tsp baking powder
Zest 1 lemon
3 medium size free-range eggs, beaten

Preheat the oven to 180°C, Gas Mark 4. Roughly chop the nuts using a large sharp knife. Put all the ingredients except the eggs into a food processor and mix together. Add the beaten eggs until the mixture forms a stiff – but not too dry – dough. You may not need all the egg so add it gradually.

Remove the dough, knead lightly until smooth, and shape into two logs, about 30cm long, 12cm wide and 2.5cm high. Lay the logs on a large non-stick baking sheet and bake for about 20 minutes, or until firm to the touch and pale gold. When the logs are cool enough to handle, take off the baking sheet and slice very thinly (about 1cm in width) on an extreme diagonal. Then return the slices to the baking sheet and pop back into the oven to bake for another 10 minutes until crisp.

Banana strudel with chocolate sauce

These little babies feel super-indulgent, but actually are far from it. The bananas provide natural sweetness and the pastry is so fine that it gives you just enough of a crispy pastry hit. It goes without saying that chocolate is a favourite of mine and something that I indulge in rather a lot (possibly too much). Drizzling over a little dark chocolate here gives you the rich chocolate flavour but without too much fat and sugar. It's been discovered that dark chocolate contains antioxidants – hurray! Another reason to tuck in.

Drizzling over a little dark chocolate here gives you the rich chocolate flavour

Serves 2
Preparation time   15 minutes
Cooking time   30 minutes

2 ripe bananas
4 sheets filo pastry
2 tsp caster sugar
Few pinches cinnamon
1 medium free-range egg, beaten
50g dark chocolate
2 tbsp low-fat crème fraîche

Preheat the oven to 180°C, Gas Mark 4. Peel and quarter the bananas lengthways, and then cut them in half again to produce sticks about 10cm long. Lay two sheets of filo on a clean chopping board and fold in half lengthways. Place half the banana sticks in the middle of the filo and sprinkle with the sugar and cinnamon. Fold in the sides and then fold the top and bottom over to envelope the banana. Repeat with the remaining filo sheets and banana.

Place both rolls join-side down on a non-stick baking sheet. Brush each with the beaten egg and bake for 20–25 minutes until golden and crisp.

Meanwhile, break up the chocolate and melt either in a small bowl in the microwave on a medium setting for 1–2 minutes, or in a heatproof bowl placed over a saucepan of gently simmering water. When the strudels are ready, remove to two plates, drizzle over the chocolate and dollop with the crème fraîche.

 Turn to page 139 for another recipe using bananas

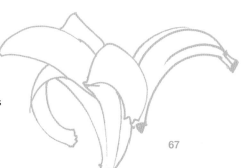

Nectarine, blueberry and raspberry with a rose water sabayon

This is a delicate, feminine dish. Sabayons are a lovely, light finish to a meal and something a little bit different. Flowers used to be used a lot in British cookery and it's a trend that's back again. This dish is very quick and easy to prepare, so I usually make it last-minute with whatever fruit and flavourings I have at hand.

A lovely, light finish to a meal and something a little bit different

Serves 2
Preparation time   10 minutes
Cooking time   15 minutes

150g raspberries
150g blueberries
1 large ripe nectarine or peach

For the sabayon
2 egg yolks
15g fruit sugar
1–2 tbsp sweet white pudding-wine
1tsp rose water

Stone the nectarine and cut into wedges but leave the raspberries and blueberries whole, and then divide the fruit between two individual serving bowls.

Put a saucepan of water on to boil. Put the egg yolks and sugar into a heatproof bowl and place on top of the saucepan. Turn the heat to a simmer and whisk the egg yolks and sugar until pale cream in colour and thick in consistency. Pour in the wine and rose water and continue whisking until the mixture is about three times its original volume.

Spoon the sabayon over each fruit portion and then glaze with a blow torch or underneath a very hot grill.

Turn to page 151 for a recipe to use any leftover egg whites

Lime and coconut surprise pudding

This is a recipe based on my great-grandmother's lemon pudding. She was a well-known cook in the 1920s and I have a beautiful old cook book from 1917, Escoffier's *A Guide to Modern Cookery*, that I love to look through. Dishes were amazingly elaborate then and, though they certainly weren't bothered about their waistlines, it's an interesting slice of history.

A recipe based on my great-grandmother's lemon pudding

Serves 4
Preparation time   20 minutes
Cooking time   40 minutes

180g fruit sugar, such as Fruisana, or 225g caster sugar
15g softened butter, plus extra for greasing dish
2 eggs, separated
Finely grated zest and juice 1 lime
2 tbsp plain flour
1 tbsp desiccated coconut
300ml half fat coconut milk
1 tbsp dried coconut shavings, optional (or extra desiccated coconut)
1 ripe mango, well chilled

Preheat the oven to 150°C, Gas Mark 3. Lightly butter a medium-size baking dish.

Beat together the sugar, butter, egg yolks, lime zest and juice until light and creamy. Stir in the flour and the desiccated coconut then beat in the coconut milk.

In a separate and very clean bowl, whisk the egg whites until stiff and then gently fold into the lime-coconut mixture. (It's important that the bowl is very clean as any grease will stop the eggs becoming stiff.) Pour the mixture into the baking dish, then sprinkle over the coconut shavings (if using) and place the dish within a larger roasting tray. Pour in enough boiling water to come halfway up the sides of the baking dish and place carefully in the oven. (This method of cooking is called bain-marie and helps the keep heat even while cooking and the sponge moist).

Bake for about 40 minutes until golden on top and springy when pressed in the centre. Peel and slice the mango. Serve the pudding hot with slices of ice-cold mango on the side.

IN-A-FLASH HEALTHY SNACKS

It's **all well and good** to say don't snack, but I have an appetite like a horse and I always find it completely impossible to avoid! As we all have so much to juggle, ladies, we need to **keep our energy levels up**. It's no excuse for diving headfirst into the fridge though, and making wise decisions is still important. Here are a **few titbits** to keep you going.

Chilli feta with pitta crisps

Chillies are great for speeding up your metabolism and I add them to a lot of my dishes. Feta is one of my favourite cheeses as it's strong and has a punchy flavour. Here I've combined the two and served them with pitta crisps. I love potato crisps, but they guarantee a year-round potbelly. Pitta crisps give you the crunch factor but aren't too fatty and making the crisps with wholemeal pittas means they are lower on the GI scale. This little snack-tastic dish is great served as part of a meze. Other dishes to make up a meze are the feta samosas [page 102], the hummus [page 76] and the lamb fillets with cumin carrots [page 166].

This little snack-tastic dish is great served as part of a meze

Serves 2
Preparation time   10 minutes
Cooking time   10 minutes

1 large fresh red chilli
Olive oil, to drizzle
200g half-fat feta, crumbled
2 spring onions
Pitta crisps, for serving

Preheat the grill. Slit the chilli down the middle, press open and pop on to a baking tray, drizzle with a little oil and grill for 10 minutes.

Let the chilli cool, then remove the stalk. Finely chop the chilli and slice the spring onions, then mix thoroughly with the feta. I keep the chilli seeds in, because I like heat, but it's up to you. Then it's ready to be served at room temperature with some pitta crisps.

 Turn to pages 38–9, 102 and 143 for more recipes featuring feta

Pitta Crisps

Serves 2 as a snack
Preparation time   5 minutes
Cooking time   5 minutes

2 wholemeal pittas
Olive oil, to drizzle
½ tsp dried oregano
Pinch chilli powder

Cut the pittas in half down the middle to separate the two sides, then cut into wedges, drizzle with the oil and sprinkle with the chilli and oregano. Toast under a hot grill then serve with the hummus dip (see page 76) or this feta dip.

Homemade oatcakes

Oatcakes are great as they are complex carbohydrates (which means they release energy slowly into your bloodstream) and are also good for anyone with a wheat allergy. I like to make my own, as then I can make sure that they don't include any flour and I also can limit unnecessary fats. Oatcakes are so simple to make and very satisfying. They taste especially delicious when fresh, but they will keep for a week or so in an airtight container.

Oatcakes are so simple to make and very satisfying

Makes about 24
Preparation time 15 minutes
Cooking time 30 minutes

250g fine oatmeal, plus extra for rolling
50g butter, at room temperature
50ml hot water, plus extra dribbles as required
½ tsp salt

Preheat the oven to 170°C, Gas Mark 3. Using your fingertips, rub together the oatmeal and butter then mix in the hot water to form a soft dough. If the mixture is too dry to form a dough, add extra hot water in dribbles until it comes together.

Sprinkle a clean worktop with extra oatmeal. Shape the dough into a smooth ball and roll out to the thickness of a £2 coin (5mm). Using a plain 6 or 7cm metal cutter, cut out as many rounds as you can, moulding the leftovers into a smaller ball and re-rolling the dough once more.

Place on a non-stick baking sheet and bake for 30 minutes until firm, then remove the tray and cool the oatcakes for 10 minutes until they crisp. Slide on to a wire rack to cool completely.

Marinated chicken pieces

Here are three different marinades for chicken pieces. I love to have cooked, flavoursome chicken pieces at the ready in the fridge for a snack on the run. Each marinade is enough for two chicken breasts and can be left on the chicken for at least an hour, but for a deeper flavour leave overnight.

A snack on the run!

Each marinade serves 2
Preparation time   10–15 minutes,
                       plus at least 1 hour for marinating
Cooking time   5 minutes

2 skinless, boneless organic chicken breasts, about
125g each, cut into pieces
Sea salt and freshly ground black pepper

One of the following marinades

Chilli, lemongrass and coconut

1 large fresh red chilli, slit
2–3cm piece fresh root ginger
1 garlic clove, crushed
1 stick lemongrass
½ tsp ground turmeric
1 tsp fish sauce
Small handful of fresh coriander
3 tbsp half fat coconut milk
Wedges of lime to serve

Blitz all the marinade ingredients together, then mix with the chicken, cover and chill for at least an hour, depending on how much time you have – overnight is ideal. Grill for 4 minutes on each side until cooked, then leave to cool. I love a little squeeze of lime over these.

Saffron, lemon and garlic

1 tbsp olive oil
Juice and zest 1 lemon
Good pinch saffron strands
2 garlic cloves, finely chopped

Gently heat up the oil and lemon juice in a small saucepan, then add the saffron, take off the heat and leave for 10 minutes to infuse and cool. Add the garlic to the saffron mix and then pour over the chicken. Marinate as before.

Preheat the grill. Season the breasts and cook for 4 minutes on each side until cooked, then allow to cool.

Maple syrup, chilli and rosemary

1 sprig of fresh rosemary, leaves only
1 garlic clove, finely chopped
1 tsp soy sauce
1 tbsp maple syrup
Pinch dried chilli flakes

Finely chop the rosemary leaves and mix with the garlic, soy sauce, maple syrup and chilli. Pour the mix over the chicken and marinate as before. Preheat the grill and cook for 4 minutes on each side until cooked, then leave to cool.

Hummus with pomegranates and pine nuts

You can buy hummus in any supermarket but it's supremely easy to make at home and best of all you'll then know exactly what's in it. Shop-bought hummus tends to contain additives and can sometimes be quite high in fat. My version has the added flavours of pine nut and pomegranates which not only makes it more exciting taste-wise, but also give it a beautiful jewel-like topping.

Serves 4
Preparation time   10 minutes
Cooking time   10 minutes

1 x 400g can chickpeas, drained
2 large cloves garlic, crushed
1 tbsp tahini
Juice 1 lemon
¼–½ tsp chilli powder, to taste
½ tsp sea salt
Freshly ground pepper
3 tbsp olive oil (reserve 1 tbsp for the topping)

For topping
1 red onion, finely sliced
1 tbsp pine nuts
½ tsp cumin seeds
½ tsp ground coriander
½ tsp cinnamon
Small handful of flat-leaf parsley, chopped
2 tbsp fresh pomegranate seeds
3 wholemeal pittas

Put all the main ingredients, 1 tbsp of oil and pepper to taste in a blender or food processor and blitz until smooth. Spoon into a serving dish and drizzle with another tbsp of oil.

Finely slice the onion and fry in the reserved tbsp of olive oil with the pine nuts for 2–3 minutes then add the spices and continue to cook for another 4–5 minutes. Spoon on top of the hummus and sprinkle with the chopped parsley.

Pop the pittas into a toaster or grill to crisp up, cut into wedges and serve along side the hummus.

How to extract pomegranate seeds
Halve a whole pomegranate and holding a half upside down whack the back of it with a large spoon or rolling pin. The seeds should fall out. Alternatively, pull them out with a teaspoon and peel off the thick membrane in between.

Social Butterfly

GLAMOROUS LIGHT-BITE CANAPÉS

Now we're talking. I have always loved canapés; I **adore** little bite-sized pieces of **taste explosions**. When I trained as a chef I took part in lots of competitions and making tiny little intricate canapés was my forte.

I often find myself at parties with an oversized piece of a carbohydrate-based canapé and that is not what you need when you're supposed to be looking your best and are wearing a dress that is completely unforgiving of anything more than a flat stomach. And, after all, it's **just not chic** to have flakes of pastry stuck to your lip gloss and how are you supposed to balance a large canapé with your glass of champagne and pretty clutch bag?

Canapés can seem fiddly to make at home and are traditionally very heavy, but there are healthier options that still impress with their taste sensations and **will make your friends jealous** of your style, grace and food! And even if the grace bit doesn't last past your second martini, the canapés will.

Coronation chicken patties with mango chutney mayo

Coronation chicken is an old summer favourite. It's terribly kitsch, of course, but like anything it can be made to perfection. Organic poached chicken, bound with good-quality spiced mayonnaise and chutney, is simply sublime. Here I have made a modern canapé version, keeping all the essential components, but updating it with a modern twist and only a small amount of mayonnaise.

Makes about 12
Preparation time   15 minutes
Cooking time   15-20 minutes

1 large fresh red chilli, deseeded and chopped
1 garlic clove, crushed
5cm piece fresh root ginger
2 skinless, boneless organic chicken breasts, roughly chopped
1 egg yolk
3 tsp mild curry powder
About 2–3 tbsp vegetable oil, for frying
Sea salt and freshly ground black pepper

For the mayonnaise
3 tbsp French-style mayonnaise
1 tbsp mango chutney, ideally the spreadable chutney without lumps
1–2 Granny Smith apples, cored and finely diced
Juice 1 lemon
3 spring onions, sliced in thin sticks
Tiny leaves from small bunch fresh coriander

Using an electric blender, briefly blitz the chilli, ginger and garlic then, with the blades running, drop in the chicken chunks and blitz briefly, using the pulse button for a chunky rough purée. Drop in the yolk, half the curry powder and seasoning to taste. Blitz to a mince consistency. Scoop out into a bowl and shape into 12 patties about 4cm diameter and 1cm high. You may find it helps to dip your hands in cold water during the shaping.

For the mayonnaise, beat the remaining curry powder with the chutney into the mayonnaise. Squeeze a little lemon juice over the apple to keep it from going brown.

Heat a frying pan until very hot and pour in a little oil. Gently fry the chicken patties for about 3 minutes on each side until firm and golden brown. Drain on a paper towel.

To serve, place the patties on to a platter in neat lines, top each patty with a spoonful of mayonnaise, slices of spring onion, cubes of apple and a tiny sprig of coriander.

Cucumber cups with wasabi tuna tartare

I love thinking of different bases for canapés. Cucumber is an obvious one and it works wonderfully here with the strong flavours of wasabi, ginger and soy. This an über-cute canapé.

This is an über-cute canapé

Makes about 24
Preparation time   20 minutes

2cm piece fresh ginger, finely grated
2 tsp soy sauce
½ tsp wasabi paste or horseradish relish
3 spring onions, finely sliced
1 cucumber
200g best tuna loin (you are eating it raw, so buy the freshest you can)
1 large fresh red chilli

Mix the wasabi, soy sauce, finely grated ginger and very finely sliced spring onions together. Thinly peel and slice the cucumber into ¾cm slices, then take a teaspoon and scoop a very shallow indentation in each slice. This will make your cup. Lay these out scooped side down on a tray in between sheets of kitchen paper to dry them off. This is very important as they are slippery when wet and also good because you can prepare them in the morning of your dinner party, well before your guests arrive.

On an EXTREMELY well-scrubbed clean board, cut the tuna into tiny cubes and pop into a bowl. Take the chilli, cut in half and discard the seeds, then cut into tiny slivers. Wash your hands in cold water afterwards as that stuff can really sting!

Just before your guests arrive, mix the soy dressing with the tuna, check the seasoning and spoon a small amount on to each slice of cucumber. Top with a sliver of chilli and serve. These look great on slate or mirror tile (mirror tiles are a bugger to keep clean, but no one said looking good was easy!).

 Turn to pages 44, 96, 109, 189 and 206 for more recipes using fresh root ginger

Pork, peanut and coriander salad cups

This is one of my eternally popular canapés, and the pork mix is great with rice or noodles too. It is based on a savoury pork Thai dish (called Galloping Horses) served on top of fruit pieces. This is a much simplified version, with a moreish combination of sweet and savoury that keeps people coming back for more.

A moreish combination of sweet and savoury

Makes 20
Preparation time   12 minutes
Cooking time   25 minutes,
  plus chilling time

2 tbsp unsalted peanuts
200g pork mince
3 garlic cloves, finely chopped
1 red chilli, slit, deseeded and finely chopped
1–2 tbsp groundnut oil (or vegetable oil)
2 tbsp palm sugar (or light muscovado sugar)
1 tbsp soy sauce
1 tbsp Thai fish sauce
Small handful fresh coriander
Small handful fresh mint
4/5 Little Gem lettuces
½ small ripe pineapple, peeled

Blitz the peanuts in a small blender to a coarse powder still with some chunks, then mix with the mince, garlic and chilli. You want all these ingredients to have the same texture so bear this in mind when chopping and blitzing.

Heat a large frying pan until very hot, add the oil and fry off the pork mixture until it starts to caramelise. This should take about 15 minutes. Then add the sugar, soy sauce and fish sauce, and cook for a further 10 minutes until you have a lovely, glossy mass. Check the seasoning, though it may not need any more salt.

Finely chop the herbs, mix them in then allow to cool. You only need the smaller inner leaves of the Little Gems, so carefully peel off the larger outer leaves (use them in a salad so they don't go to waste!). Trim off the stalks so you are left with leaves like cute little Chinese spoons. Spoon the filling into the 'bowl' of the lettuce spoons and chill lightly until set.

Chop the pineapple into small dice, spoon on top of the mince and serve.

Bloody Mary oyster shots

The best opening to a New Year's party: fresh oysters in a Bloody Mary. Choose quite small oysters (ideally small 'natives' or *Fine de Claire*, but the craggy Pacific oysters are also good). Oysters are best opened just before they are consumed, although it can be difficult to do. See my method below or buy an oyster-cracking tool.

The best opening to a New Year's party

Makes 20
Preparation time   20 minutes

1 litre V8 vegetable juice
200ml good quality vodka (Grey Goose is my favourite)
2 tbsp Worcestershire sauce
Juice 1 lemon
Tabasco to taste
20 fresh oysters
Sea salt and freshly ground black pepper

Mix all the Bloody Mary liquids together, adding Tabasco in little shakes and tasting as you go. Chill in a jug until you're ready to open the oysters.

Take 20 shot glasses and spread them out on a tray. Open the oysters, strain any oyster juice into the Bloody Mary mix and pop an oyster into each glass. Pour the mix over the oysters and serve immediately, well chilled.

How to open (shuck) oysters

Firstly, fold a clean tea towel twice lengthways and wrap it around your left hand (or right if you are left-handed). Hold an oyster firmly in the wrapped hand with the flat shell on top and hinge pointing outwards.

Using a stubby oyster knife, work the point of the knife into the hinge, wriggling it until the oyster inside relaxes and releases the seal. Then push the knife further in and swipe it across the inside to loosen the small muscle that holds the meat to the shell.

You should then be able to lift off the top shell. Ideally tip any juice into a small jug or bowl. Slide the knife along the bottom of the second shell to loosen the oyster completely. Fresh oysters should be eaten immediately, but if needed you can shuck them about half an hour ahead and store them in their juice in the fridge.

Manchego, Membrillo and Serrano ham skewers

Quince jelly (membrillo) is a sweet, aromatic fruit paste that is traditionally served with cheese in Spain. Here I've paired it with the classic Manchego cheese, but it works very well with blue cheese or even a softer goats' cheese. These little canapés can be made in the morning and just brought up to room temperature before the guests arrive. They go down very well! If you can't find membrillo then fig, pear or apple jelly also works well.

Makes about 20
Preparation time 15 minutes

200g Manchego cheese (or even your favourite blue cheese, I love the tanginess of Roquefort)
4 slices of Serrano ham
150g quince jelly (membrillo)

Cut the cheese into small rectangular cubes about 2.5cm long and 1cm wide. Cut the Serrano ham in half, first lengthways and then in half across.

This gives you perfect strips to wrap around the cheese. Neatly wrap each piece of cheese and trim any jagged edges. Cut the membrillo into cubes the same size as the cheese and skewer on top of the little ham parcels with wooden cocktail sticks. Then serve!

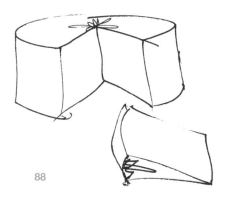

Blackened-salmon and mango tartlets

These are colourful little tartlets that are full of flavour: canapés are small so the flavours need to be big! Using salmon, spices and sweet mango really gets the taste buds going. I have used filo pastry, as it has that delicate thinness and crispy texture, without any stodginess. These are beautiful canapés that would easily grace any glamorous soirée.

Salmon, spices and sweet mango really get the taste buds going

Makes 24
Preparation time   25 minutes
Cooking time   10 minutes

250g salmon fillet, cut into four large chunks
12 filo pastry sheets, about 30x20cm
1 tbsp olive oil
1 mango, peeled and finely diced
1 red chilli, slit, deseeded and finely diced
1 red onion, finely diced
Juice 1 lime
Small handful coriander, chopped
50g jar salmon keta (aka salmon eggs or salmon caviar, optional)
Sea salt and freshly ground black pepper

For the spice mix
1 tsp paprika, ideally smoked
½ tsp ground cumin
½ tsp ground coriander
½ tsp dried oregano
½ tsp cayenne pepper
½ tsp allspice
½ tsp garlic powder
Sea salt and freshly ground black pepper

Combine all the spice mix ingredients and use to completely coat the salmon. Chill the spiced salmon while you make the tartlets.

Preheat the oven to 180°C, Gas Mark 4. Unroll the filo sheets and keep them covered with a clean damp tea towel or sheet of clingfilm when you're not using them. Take 1 sheet of pastry, brush lightly with oil and sandwich with another sheet on top. Cut these two sandwiched sheets into 10cm wide strips and then cut each strip into 10cm squares. Take two squares and press together – setting one square at an angle to the other to make a star or crown shape with 8 points. This will make one tartlet case. Brush this lightly with more oil and repeat with the rest of the filo squares until you've used all your filo sheets. Press each shape into the wells of little muffin tins and bake for about 15 minutes until crisp and golden. Leave to cool on a wire rack. (Note: you may need to bake in two batches, depending on how many you make.)

Mix together the diced mango, chilli and onion with the lime juice, coriander and seasoning to form a salsa. Put to one side.

Heat a non-stick frying pan until extremely hot. Add a trickle of oil and swirl around the pan. Fry the salmon, getting it as 'blackened' or well chargrilled as possible (without it actually burning) for lots of flavour. You don't want to overcook it though, so keep it a little pink inside. Leave to cool.

To serve, break up into manageable chunks and place in the filo cases. Top with some salsa and some salmon eggs, if using.

Glam Gourmet rarebit

Rarebit is a truly classic Welsh recipe, and there are lots of different versions of this dish. My Glamorous Gourmet rarebit puts dark rye bread against the white goats' cheese with what else but bubbles! The beauty of pumpernickel is that it isn't wheat-based so won't make you feel so bloated and is higher on the GI index than bread. Enjoy this dish and be a true glamorous gourmet.

Enjoy this dish and be a true glamorous gourmet

Makes 20
Preparation time   10 minutes
Cooking time   10–15 minutes

250g hard goats' cheese, grated
50g soft goats' cheese (rindless)
1 tsp Dijon or French mustard
75ml/5 tbsp sparkling wine
1 free-range egg yolk
6 slices German- or Swedish-style rye or
pumpernickel bread (this can be found in most
shops and supermarkets)
4 tbsp caramelised red-onion marmalade,
homemade or shop-bought

Mix the two goats' cheeses, mustard, egg yolk and wine to a paste in a bowl. Toast the bread on both sides under a hot grill. Spread a little onion marmalade on the toast, then spoon on the goats' cheese mixture.

Pop back under the grill and cook until golden and bubbling. Leave to cool for 1 minute, then cut into small 3cm squares and serve!

Turn to page 94 for another recipe using goats' cheese

Rare roast beef with truffle oil and Parmesan

This is another one of my carb-free specials. Rare roast beef wrapped around watercress and Parmesan – all flavour and all good! I love the rich, earthy scent of truffle and can't get enough of it, especially when it's combined with classic watercress, beef and cheese. These disappear very quickly though, so make plenty.

Another one of my carb-free specials

Makes 20
Preparation time 10 minutes
Cooking time 20 minutes

500g tail-end beef fillet
1 tbsp olive oil
Truffle-flavoured olive oil, for drizzling
1 bunch watercress (or 100g pack)
75g fresh Parmesan shavings
Sea salt and freshly ground black pepper

Preheat the oven to 200°C, Gas Mark 6. To cook the beef, heat a heavy-based non-stick frying pan until piping hot. Season the beef well. Add the oil to the pan and swirl around to coat the pan evenly. Add the beef and cook for about 5–7 minutes, turning two to three times until nicely browned. Remove and place in a small roasting pan. Roast for 10 minutes then remove and leave to cool for a good 15 minutes.

Using a razor-sharp carving knife, slice the beef as thinly into rounds as possible – it should be lovely and pink in the middle. Place on a large plate and drizzle with the carving juices and about a tablespoon of truffle oil.

Pick the watercress into lovely little sprigs. Place a few sprigs on to each beef slice, add a small shaving of cheese and roll up. Arrange on a platter, drizzle with more truffle oil and scatter over more Parmesan slices. Serve at room temperature garnished with any leftover watercress sprigs.

Chinese spoons with cauliflower purée, crispy monkfish and wild mushrooms

Serving mini morsels on Chinese spoons never fails to please guests. You can serve a range of different ingredients and really push the limits of canapés: for example, risotto, mini ravioli and even mini bangers and mash all look great served in a Chinese spoon. The cauliflower purée is a beautiful, snow-like colour and, if you can find the trompette noir mushrooms, the visual contrast is fantastic. This recipe works well with different combinations, too; scallops would be good alternatives to monkfish.

Mini morsels on Chinese spoons never fails to please guests

Makes 20
Preparation time   20 minutes
Cooking time   15 minutes,
                         plus cooling time

1 medium head cauliflower (make sure
it is very fresh)
500ml milk
200ml chicken stock (can be made with a cube
or bouillon powder)
1 clove garlic, crushed
400g monkfish fillet (ask the fishmonger to
remove all the skin and pinky grey membrane)
200g wild mushrooms, cleaned of grit and torn
roughly (ideally trompette noir or girolles but
chestnut mushrooms will do)
Small handful tarragon leaves, roughly chopped
25g butter
2 tbsp olive oil
Squeeze lemon
Sea salt and freshly ground black pepper

Quarter the cauliflower and cut out most of the core, then shave or slice the cauliflower as thinly as possible so it cooks quickly. Place in a saucepan with the milk, stock, garlic and some seasoning. Bring to the boil and simmer for 5–6 minutes then remove from the heat. Leave to cool in the liquid for 15 minutes.

Meanwhile, cut the monkfish into 20 bite-sized cubes and the mushrooms into slightly smaller pieces. Roughly chop the tarragon.

Drain the cauliflower and blitz in a food processor or blender until very smooth. For the ultimate silky purée, rub the mixture through a sieve with the back of a ladle. Beat in the butter and check the seasoning. Set aside.

Heat a frying pan, add a trickle of oil and fry the monkfish for about 5 minutes, stirring and tossing until golden brown. Season and tip on to a plate. In the same pan, add remaining oil and heat until very hot. Pan-fry the sliced mushrooms for around 5–6 minutes. Season, add the tarragon and a squeeze of lemon.

Arrange 20 Chinese soup spoons (or your best dessert spoons) on a platter or tray. Place a little purée on each spoon, top with a piece of monkfish and some mushrooms.

Parma ham- and goats'-cheese-wrapped asparagus with nectarine and pink peppercorn dip

Simple flavours and textures always work well: I adore asparagus in season and with the goats' cheese and Parma ham it tastes simply divine. The nectarines make a beautiful pink dip and the whole effect is stunning when served at a party.

The nectarines make a beautiful pink dip

Makes 20
Preparation time   15 minutes
Cooking time   20 minutes

20 asparagus tips
20 Parma ham
150g rindless goats' cheese, crumbled

For the dip
5 nectarines
1 tsp cracked pink peppercorns
2 tbsp white balsamic vinegar
1 tbsp fruit sugar

Trim the ends of the asparagus. Cut each slice of ham in half widthways. Crumble a little cheese in the centre of a slice of the Parma ham and place an asparagus tip on top. Wrap up firmly and place join-side down on a non-stick baking tray. Repeat this process with each Parma ham slice. Set the tray of little parcels to one side.

To make the dip, score the nectarines in half and twist to separate. Remove the stones from the fruit. Chop the flesh into 1cm cubes. Place the nectarine cubes, vinegar, sugar and peppercorns in a saucepan with 3 tablespoons of water. Bring to the boil, then reduce the heat and stir as it simmers for 15 minutes, until thick. Chill the mixture in the fridge.

Just before your guests arrive, cook the asparagus under a grill for about 5–8 minutes until crisp and golden brown. Drain on paper towels and leave to cool slightly. Serve while still warm on a platter with the dip in a bowl.

Turn to pages 158, 162–3 and 200 for more recipes using asparagus

SLEEK AND SLENDER DINNER PARTY DISHES

The words 'dinner party' can sound old-fashioned and out-dated, but there is **no greater pleasure** than cooking for friends. There is something very caring and beautiful in taking time to prepare your ingredients and produce food for loved ones. It is really a sign of affection, and a gift for everyone. I know that some of that joy can be lost when cooking for a family (or even for work, like me) but hopefully these recipes will **ignite your love of cooking** again and you'll cherish the process as much as the event.

No running around like a sweaty lunatic and hitting the cooking wine, though – a friend of mine recently went to a dinner party and said that you could hear the hostess sobbing in the kitchen by the main course. This is not a good look! **Don't forget, your friends are there to enjoy your sparkling wit more than the food**, so don't take it too seriously.

STARTERS

Shiitake and smoked chicken broth

Another delicious, nourishing soup. Braising the dried mushrooms to make the rich stock-base really gives the broth some depth. I tend to theme my dinner party menus and this has a Chinese feel to it, so keep that in mind when planning the rest of the menu. Despite its grown-up flavour, it is very light so will go down well with figure-conscious friends.

Another delicious, nourishing soup

Serves 4
Preparation time   20 minutes
Cooking time   40 minutes

50g dried shiitake mushrooms
50g other dried Chinese mushrooms or dried porcini mushrooms
1 fresh red chilli, slit lengthways
5cm piece fresh root ginger, thickly sliced
5 spring onions, roughly chopped
1 tbsp soy sauce
1.5 litres chicken stock (can be made with a stock cube or bouillon powder)

To serve
50g rice vermicelli noodles or thin egg noodles
2 small smoked chicken breasts,
skinned and diced
2 spring onions, finely sliced
Small handful coriander leaves, roughly chopped

Place all the broth ingredients, from the dried mushrooms to the stock, into a saucepan and bring to the boil. Turn down and simmer for 40 minutes. Strain the liquid into another saucepan and reserve the shiitake mushrooms (the other ingredients can be discarded).

Slice the shiitakes and return to the pan with the stock and add the noodles. Leave to soak in the hot stock for 20 minutes.

Divide the sliced onions and diced chicken between 4 soup bowls. Reheat the broth and mushrooms and when simmering pour into the bowls. Serve topped with the chopped coriander and a wedge of lime, if available.

Turn to pages 44, 82, 109 and 206 for more recipes using fresh root ginger

Curried potted mackerel with apple salad

Traditionally, the English love potted fish and curry spices, and for good reason – they work so well together. This is an old-fashioned dish that your guests will love. It is also very easy to make the day before, so you can serve with ease! It's great with hot toast or just the salad. It's also ideal as a healthy Omega 3 oil-packed snack to leave in the fridge.

This is an old-fashioned dish that your guests will love

Serves 4
Preparation time   5 minutes
Cooking time   10 minutes

250–300g smoked mackerel fillets, skinned
2 shallots, diced
Pinch mace
2 tsp curry powder
1 tbsp olive oil
Small bunch chives, finely sliced
Zest and juice 1 lemon
1 tbsp reduced-fat soured cream
1 crisp red apple
1 crisp green apple
1 tsp coarse-grain mustard
Pinch cayenne
Picked watercress sprigs, to serve
Sea salt and freshly ground black pepper

Skin the mackerel and place the flesh in a big bowl, discarding the skin. Flake with a fork. In a little pan, sweat the shallots, mace and curry powder in the oil for about 5 minutes until translucent.

Tip the curried shallots into the bowl of mackerel along with the lemon zest, chives and soured cream. Mix well and check the seasoning, then either pop into individual ramekins or into a large dish. Chill the mix in the fridge.

Quarter and core the apples, then cut into little batons and dress with a squeeze of lemon, the mustard and cayenne. Serve in the ramekins or, if in a large dish, scoop out the fish mixture in oval quenelles or neat, round mounds. Serve with posies of watercress and hot rye toast.

Chicken liver pâté with Armagnac prunes

This dish truly highlights the difference between shop-bought and homemade: there is no comparison! It's so quick to make, so tasty, so good – and not bulked up with fat like the shop-bought stuff. Let me set the scene for you: loads of friends; a big dish of smooth, rich pâté with the sweet, glazed prunes and apple, and good wine. Now we're talking proper food.

It's so quick to make, so tasty, so good

Serves 6
Preparation time   30 minutes, plus marinating and setting time
Cooking time   15 minutes

100g no-need-to-soak prunes, stoned and chopped
100ml Armagnac
500g organic chicken livers
25g butter
2 tbsp olive oil
1 large shallot, chopped
3 cloves garlic, chopped
1 tsp sage leaves, chopped
2 sprigs of thyme, leaves removed
3 tbsp single cream
1 tbsp redcurrant jelly
Sea salt and freshly ground black pepper

For the topping
1 dessert apple, such as Cox or Granny Smith
1 tbsp walnut oil
1 tsp fruit sugar

Chop the prunes into small dice and marinate for an hour in half the Armagnac. Trim any fatty or bloody bits off the livers and cut into small, even-sized pieces. Using a large non-stick frying pan, gently sauté the shallot and garlic in the butter and oil for about 5 minutes until softened and translucent. Then add the chicken livers and cook for 5 minutes, turning occasionally. Make sure to keep them pink in the middle.

Season the livers then stir in the remaining Armagnac, cream, herbs and redcurrant jelly and cook for 2–3 minutes. Check the seasoning again – remember that when food is served cold (as this pâté will be) the seasoning and flavours are muted, so you can be relatively bold.

Blitz the livers and pan juices to a smooth paste in a food processor or blender. Divide the paste between six ramekins or spoon into a medium-size dish or 500g loaf tin. Leave to cool and then chill.

To make the apple and prune topping, peel, core and cut the apple into small neat dice. Heat a frying pan and add the walnut oil, then the diced apple. Fry until lightly browned then sprinkle over the sugar. Cook the apple for about 5 minutes until tender, but still holding a good shape. Add the prunes and cook for a further few minutes until the alcohol evaporates away. Then remove and cool.

Spoon on top of the pâtés, patting down gently to firm, and return to chill until set. Serve with celery sticks (for those who don't eat bread) or crispy toast (wholegrain, rye or sourdough is best) or – if you are being a little naughty – rich, toasted brioche.

Prawn Ceviche

Ceviche is a great, fresh way to start a meal and get your taste buds tingling. The fish is essentially 'cooked' by the lime juice, so the ingredients need to be very fresh. The popcorn sounds weird, but it is actually a traditional accompaniment and the textures are somehow fun together.

A great, fresh way to start a meal and get your taste buds tingling

Serves 4
Preparation time   20 minutes, plus 2 hours
chilling time

500g raw king prawns, shelled and cleaned, well thawed if using frozen
1 small papaya, not too ripe
200g yellow or red cherry tomatoes halved
½ red onion, thinly sliced
1 red chilli, slit lengthways, deseeded and diced finely
100g canned palm hearts (optional), drained and sliced
Juice 4 limes
100ml fresh orange juice
Small handful coriander leaves, chopped
Good pinch fruit sugar
Sea salt and freshly ground pepper

To serve
Popcorn (optional)
Pinch cayenne pepper
4 Martini glasses

Bring a saucepan of water to the boil, remove from the heat and add the prawns. Leave to stand for 40 seconds and then drain. Refresh the prawns under cold running water. Pat dry with a paper towel.

Halve, deseed and peel the papaya then cut into fine dice, about 5mm in size. Mix the papaya with the tomatoes, onion, chilli, palm hearts (if using), lime and orange juice. Pour this mixture over the prawns. Cover and chill for two hours. (The citrus juices help to 'cook' the prawns.)

Remove from the fridge. Drain the juice from the mixture and reserve 2–3 tablespoons of it. Place this juice in a bowl and add the chopped coriander, a pinch of sugar and a pinch of salt to make a dressing.

To make chilli popcorn, add a pinch of cayenne pepper to a bag of plain or salted popcorn and shake it up so the cayenne gets dispersed and colours the popcorn slightly. Add more than a pinch of cayenne if you like it spicy. Spoon the prawns into four chilled Martini (or wine) glasses, spoon over the dressing and serve with the popcorn on the side.

How I prepare raw prawns
To de-vein raw prawns, score the curled tops with the tip of a sharp knife and scrape out the dark intestinal line.

Cumin, feta and mango chutney samosas

Strange though the ingredients list may seem, these are the most moreish little devils. They get quickly demolished whenever I make them. The samosas are a lovely little vegetarian dish or you can make smaller versions for canapés and meze platters.

These are the most moreish little devils

Serves 8
Preparation time 5 minutes
Cooking time 20 minutes

2 tsp cumin seeds
150g reduced-fat feta cheese, crumbled
1 bunch spring onions, finely sliced
2 tsp mango chutney
4 sheets filo pastry
Olive oil, for brushing
Freshly ground black pepper

Preheat the oven to 190°C, Gas Mark 5. In a dry frying pan, heat the cumin seeds until they begin to give off an aroma. In a bowl, mix together the crumbled feta, cumin seeds, spring onion and mango chutney. Season with pepper – the mix won't need any salt because of the flavour of the feta.

Stack the filo sheets on top of each other and cut into 8 strips about 7cm wide. Spoon a little of the feta mix on the corner of one strip. Fold the corner over to form a triangle at the end of the strip. Fold it over again and again, always on the diagonal, until you end up with a triangular parcel or samosa.

Repeat with the remaining feta and filo. Place on a non-stick baking sheet and brush lightly with olive oil. Bake for 15 minutes or until golden brown and crisp. Serve with a green salad and, if you like, some yogurt mixed with chopped fresh mint (see my recipe for masala eggs, page 132).

Turn to pages 38–9, 73 and 143 for more recipes using feta

Portobello mushrooms with chestnut duxelle and brioche

Portobello mushrooms are beautiful large, meaty mushrooms and make the base of a brilliant vegetarian meal. The chestnut and mushroom filling is also earthy in flavour and the brioche adds a sweet crispiness.

Beautiful large, meaty mushrooms

Serves 4
Preparation time   15 minutes
Cooking time   25 minutes

8 Portobello mushrooms, peeled
2 shallots, finely chopped
2 cloves garlic, finely chopped
250g chestnut mushrooms, roughly chopped
50g butter
100g cooked, peeled chestnuts (these can be from vacuum pack), roughly chopped
1 sprig thyme
1 tbsp chopped parsley
200g baby leaf spinach
2 tablespoons olive oil
2 slices of brioche, or country-style bread
Sea salt and freshly ground black pepper

Fry the shallots, garlic and mushrooms in the butter for about 5 minutes until softened. You want a little colour on the mushrooms but take care not to burn the onions and garlic. Add the chestnuts, thyme, parsley and spinach. Stir until the spinach leaves wilt. Season and take the pan off the heat.

Preheat the oven to 200°C, Gas Mark 6. Place the Portobello mushrooms in a baking dish, drizzle with 2 tbsp of olive oil and season. Pile some of the chestnut filling into the centre of each mushroom.

Trim off the crusts from the brioche then dice into cubes slightly smaller than 1cm. Sprinkle the cubes over the mushrooms. Bake for 20 minutes until the mushrooms are tender. This dish is great served with lightly buttered vegetables.

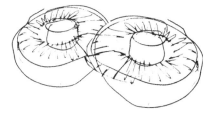

Turn to page 31 for another recipe using chestnuts

103

MAIN COURSES

Redcurrant-glazed venison with celeriac gratin and wilted Savoy cabbage

Venison should be kept pink, like other meats that are low in fat, as this keeps the flavour. Gratins are always very popular and this version made with celeriac is a decidedly more delicate affair than the usual, with a fantastic flavour.

Serves 4
Preparation time   1 hour
Cooking time   75 minutes

2 small celeriac, about 300g each (if you can't find small ones, a large celeriac of about 600g is fine)
250ml stock (can be made with a cube)
25g butter
1 garlic clove, crushed
1 sprig thyme
½ Savoy cabbage, outer leaves removed
4 tbsp olive oil
1 onion, sliced thinly
2 tbsp reduced-fat crème fraîche
1 large tsp wholegrain mustard
4 venison steaks, about 125g each
150ml red wine
1 tbsp redcurrant jelly
Sea salt and freshly ground black pepper

Lightly grease a square baking tin (about 15cm square) with a little oil. Preheat the oven to 180°C, Gas Mark 4.

The celeriac can be prepared and cooked ahead of time, if necessary. Peel the celeriac and slice thinly, ideally on a mandolin or Japanese food slicer. Heat up the stock with the garlic clove, butter and the sprig of thyme. Put the celeriac slices into a bowl and pour over the hot stock. Leave until cool enough to handle then drain the stock into a jug. Put the stock aside.

Layer the celeriac in the baking tray. Press it right down so it's very compact. Pour over half of the reserved stock and cover the tray with foil. Pop the celeriac in the oven and cook for 40 minutes, then take off the foil and cook for a further 20 minutes or brown under a hot grill. When it's cooked, remove from the oven and leave to cool. Press down on the celeriac again to make sure it's really compact. Remove from the baking dish and cut into wedges. Pop the wedges on to another baking sheet and leave, ready to reheat for 10 minutes while cooking the venison.

Cut out the core from the cabbage and shred the rest finely. Heat 1 tbsp of oil in a medium saucepan and cook the onion for about 5 minutes until softened and translucent. Add the cabbage and 4 tbsp of water and some seasoning and continue to cook for 5 minutes. Then stir in the crème fraîche and mustard. Do not completely cook the cabbage as you want to reheat it later and don't want to overcook then.

A decidedly more delicate affair than the usual

Reheat the celeriac gratin in the oven for 10 minutes. Now cook the venison. Heat a heavy-based frying pan, add a tablespoon of oil and season the venison steaks. Carefully place the steaks in the pan. Cook for about 3 minutes on each side (venison should never be overcooked). Remove from the pan and pop on to a plate. Stir the red wine and redcurrant jelly into the pan juices and simmer for 2 minutes until glossy. Take the pan off the heat and put the venison back in. Cover the steaks in the glaze and leave to rest for 5 minutes.

Place a wedge of gratin and a mound of cabbage on each warmed plate. Slice the venison and lay on top. Drizzle over the pan juices. Lovely!

Rack of lamb with caponata-stuffed tomatoes and olive oil mash

This recipe is a little bit cheffy, but doesn't show off too much. The flavours are simple and a classic combination. Rack of lamb is very tender and the stuffed, deeply colourful tomato petals look beautiful. This is really a dish to impress people with, but even with entertaining in mind I try to make food healthier. So it's out with all the butter and cream usually found in mash, and in with olive oil and sweet roasted garlic. The flavour is still brilliant and you don't miss a thing.

Serves 6
Preparation time   30 minutes
Cooking time   1 hour

3 large plum tomatoes
3 lamb racks (with six bones on each rack),
French trimmed (only the scraped rib bones left in)
6 tbsp olive oil
Sea salt and freshly ground black pepper

For the mash
1.5kg potatoes (King Edward or Maris Piper),
peeled and cut in equal-size chunks
1 whole bulb garlic

For the caponata
1 medium aubergine
2 medium courgettes
1 red onion, halved
2 sticks celery
1 yellow pepper, cored and deseeded
2 tsp balsamic vinegar
Pinch salt and sugar
100ml tomato passata (use any left over in one of
the hangover cures on page 127)
25g toasted pine nuts

**For the pesto dressing (This makes enough
for one dinner party and two pasta suppers
after that – it freezes well)**
25g pine nuts, toasted
100g fresh Parmesan, grated
50g fresh basil, including stalks
1 garlic clove, chopped

Heat the oven to 190°C, Gas Mark 5. To make the mash, wrap the whole garlic bulb in a sheet of foil and roast for 40–45 minutes until softened. Leave to cool, still wrapped in foil. Peel the potatoes and cut into equal-sized pieces. Boil in lightly salted water for 15–20 minutes or until just tender. Drain and return to the saucepan.

Unwrap the garlic and separate the cloves from the skin of the bulb. Put the peeled cloves in a cup and mash with a fork to a purée. If you want to be an ultra purist, put the cloves into a sieve and rub through with a wooden spoon. Mash the potatoes until smooth (don't use a food processor or blender as this will make the potatoes too gluey) then mix in the garlic and a tablespoon of oil. Check the seasoning and set aside for later.

To make the caponata, cut all the vegetables into small-size dice, about 5mm–1cm big. Try not to include the pale centres of the courgette and aubergine.

Heat 2 tbsp olive oil in a medium saucepan and add the onion and aubergine. Cook for a couple of minutes on a high heat and then add the diced courgettes, peppers and celery. Cook for a further 8 minutes, stirring occasionally, and then add the tomato passata, vinegar and seasoning. Cook for 10–15 minutes until rich and thickened. Add the pine nuts. Set the caponata aside.

Cut the plum tomatoes into quarters then, using a sharp knife, cut out all the seeds, so you have boat-shaped petals. Spoon some of the caponata on top of each petal.

To make the pesto, blitz all the ingredients together in a food processor until smooth. Reserve a third for this dish and thin down a little by adding a tablespoon of

This is really a dish to impress people with

water. Pour the remaining two thirds into a small jar or food container to chill or freeze. Now you can cook the racks. Trim them of excess fat and cut each rack in half by slicing lengthways down between the chops. Preheat the oven to 200°C, Gas Mark 6. Heat a large non-stick frying pan and add a tablespoon of olive oil. Sear the lamb on all sides until nicely brown. Place the lamb in a roasting pan, season and cook along with the tomato petals for about 10 minutes. After this time, the lamb should feel a little springy when pressed with the back of a fork. Remove and leave to cool for 5 minutes before cutting each half-rack into three chops.

While the lamb is cooking, reheat the mash in the oven and check the seasoning. Spoon the mash into the centre of warmed dinner plates and arrange the lamb chops on top, with the stuffed tomato petals placed around. Finally, drizzle over the pesto and serve.

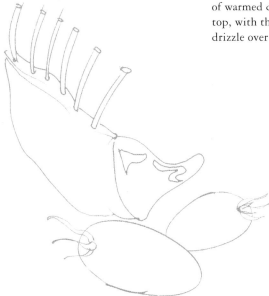

Roasted duck with star-anise pears

Kohlrabis are funny little UFO-like vegetables. They make great potato replacements for fondants, and are slightly more exotic. The duck is fantastic with the five-spice rub and star-anise pears – it uses eastern and western flavours together. The pears are good enough to be served separately as a pudding with ice cream too!

Serves 4
Preparation time   35 minutes
Cooking time   70 minutes

4 duck breasts, about 150g each
1 tsp five-spice powder
2 Asian pears
100g fruit sugar
5cm piece fresh root ginger
2 star anise
1 tsp Szechwan peppercorns
4 small or 1 large kohlrabi (if you can't find kohlrabi then use 2 medium turnips)
1 tbsp sesame oil
500ml vegetable stock (can be made from a cube)
4 small heads bok choi
2 tbsp soy sauce

Score the skin of the duck breasts, rub with five-spice powder and set aside.

Peel, quarter and core the pears, keeping their shape as much as possible. Put the sugar, 300ml of water, ginger, star anise and peppercorns into a saucepan and bring to the boil. Add the pears and simmer for about 10 minutes or until just tender.

Peel the kohlrabi and using a round cutter cut into 4 neat circles. This is not essential but makes the dish look smart! Alternatively, if you are using 1 large kohlrabi then cut into four thick slices.

In a non-stick frying pan, heat the sesame oil. Add the kohlrabi and brown on each side. Add the stock to the pan and cover with greaseproof paper (wet the paper and scrunch it around the edges so it has a better fit). Cook for about 30 to 35 minutes on a very low heat until tender and most of the stock has evaporated.

Put another frying pan on a very low heat. Season the duck breasts and place skin-side down in the pan. Cook slowly for about 15 minutes, periodically draining off the fat into a bowl. This slow cooking is to render the fat from the skin, so don't worry that the duck isn't browning off. After the 15 minutes is up, turn up the heat and now brown off the fat-side of the duck. Turn the breasts over and cook on the flesh side for a few minutes to brown. Remove from the pan and leave to rest for 10 minutes.

While the duck is resting, put a pan of water on to boil. Steam the bok choi and cook for 5 minutes using a steamer basket. Remove from the basket and sprinkle with the soy sauce. Reheat the pears.

To serve, place the kohlrabi and bok choi on the plate. Slice the duck into medallions and arrange on top of the vegetables. Sit two pear quarters on each plate.

To make this easier to prepare for dinner parties, poach the pears the day before and cook the kohlrabi a few hours before, then just reheat both last-minute.

Vine-leaf wrapped chicken with ricotta, pine nut and mint stuffing

I was in Mykonos last summer and wanted to make a dinner from local ingredients but that would be different from food found on local menus. Vine leaves are used a lot in Greek cooking and wrapping them around the chicken keeps it really moist. The mint and pine nuts add texture and flavour and look great. Looking out over the sparkling blue bay and whitewashed walls, this was a memorable meal for me, and I hope it will be for you too!

Serves 4
Preparation time   25 minutes
Cooking time   30–35 minutes

250g reduced-fat ricotta cheese or the Greek cheese called Mizithra
50g toasted pine nuts
50g sultanas
3 tbsp fresh mint leaves, chopped
Zest one lemon
4 free-range skinless boneless chicken breasts, about 125g each
12 vine leaves (these can be bought in jars in good delis or some supermarkets)
Sea salt and freshly ground black pepper

To serve
1 red onion, thinly sliced
1 fistful picked flat-leaf parsley leaves
2 tbsp olive oil
1–2 tbsp lemon juice
1 large aubergine
2 garlic cloves, thickly sliced

Preheat the oven to 200°C, Gas Mark 6. Mix the ricotta, sultanas, pine nuts, chopped mint leaves, lemon zest and seasoning together.

To prepare the onion salad, mix the onion slices with the picked whole parsley leaves and the oil and lemon juice. Season and set aside while you cook the chicken.

Place the chicken breasts on a very clean board and, using a sharp knife, cut through the middle horizontally, but not right through. This will make a butterfly shape when the chicken breast is opened up. Press a quarter of the ricotta filling in the centre of a breast and fold the top flap of flesh to sandwich together like a sub roll.

Lay out 3 vine leaves so they overlap slightly. Place a stuffed chicken breast on top and fold in the sides to enclose, then roll up tightly to form a cylinder-shaped roll. Place join-side down in a shallow baking dish. Repeat with the other 3 breasts. Season lightly, cover loosely with foil and bake for 30–35 minutes until they feel firm when pressed with the back of a fork. Remove and leave to stand while you cook the aubergines.

Preheat a griddle pan until hot. Slice the aubergine into 1cm slices. Slice the garlic lengthways and rub on to both sides of the aubergine. Brush the aubergines lightly with olive oil and season. Cook the garlic-flavoured aubergines for 4–5 minutes on each side, getting lots of colour and making sure they cook right through. There is nothing worse than undercooked aubergine!

Arrange the aubergine slices on warmed plates. Slice each chicken breast in half on the diagonal and place on top of the aubergines. Spoon the onion around the chicken and serve.

DESERTS

Stem ginger crème brûlée with lychee salad

Stem ginger has a jewel-like quality and adds an aromatic spiciness to dishes. Lychees are translucent and glossy, and their pureness works well in this dish. Crème brûlées are usually a little naughty as they are extremely creamy, but my recipe is a much healthier take on the traditional.

My recipe is a much healthier take on the traditional

Makes 8
Preparation time 15 minutes
Cooking time   35 minutes

150ml double cream
500ml milk
60g stem ginger (roughly 4 knobs),
plus 2 tbsp of the syrup
1 vanilla pod, split
8 free-range egg yolks
50g fruit sugar
1 x 400g can of lychees, in syrup, drained
1 small cantaloupe melon
75g demerara sugar

Heat the oven to 170°C, Gas Mark 3. Put the cream, milk and ginger syrup in a non-stick saucepan. Scrape out the sticky seeds from the vanilla pod and add to the milk along with the pod. Bring slowly to just below boiling point, but be careful not to let it boil over.

Beat the yolks with the fruit sugar in a large heatproof bowl, then whisk in the hot milk. Strain through a fine sieve into a jug.

Lay out 8 ramekins in a large shallow roasting pan. Slice the ginger knobs finely and divide between the bases of the ramekins. Pour the custard on top. Then boil a large kettle of water and pour into the pan, around each ramekin, so that the water reaches halfway up the sides of the ramekins.

Carefully place the roasting pan of ramekins in the oven and bake for 30–35 minutes until the crème brûlées feel slightly firm but with a slight wobble to them when pushed. Carefully remove the pan, taking care not to spill the very hot water, and leave the ramekins to cool for 10 minutes before lifting them out of the pan and setting aside to cool completely.

Scoop little balls of flesh from the melon (this looks so tacky it's fun!). Halve the lychees and mix with the melon. Chill in the fridge. Sprinkle the tops of the brûlées with the sugar and caramelise with a blow torch until golden brown. If you don't have a blow torch, heat under a red-hot grill. Leave to cool and for the tops to crisp up. Serve the crème brûlées with the fruit salad on the side.

Blood orange and grenadine jellies

Wonderful, wobbling, colourful jellies. Inside everyone is a small child with a passion for jelly: make these for a kid's party and it will be the adults who grab the plates first. Jellies are great for slimline diets as you get a sweet hit without too many calories. I am sure we can tell ourselves that we get some vitamins from the fruit juice, too.

These jellies are also very versatile, and can look sophisticated at dinner parties. I often make champagne and peach jellies or elderflower and blackberry versions. If you're determined to be naughty, add a few vodka shots to the mix . . .

Inside everyone is a small child with a passion for jelly

Serves 4
Preparation time 15 minutes, plus 3 hours setting time
Cooking time 5 minutes

2 sheets leaf gelatine
400ml blood-orange juice (juice from a carton is fine – Tropicana sanguinello is good)
3 tbsp grenadine syrup
2 oranges

Put the gelatine into a bowl and cover with cold water, then leave to one side until softened and floppy.

Gently heat 150ml of the orange juice, until it's just below boiling point. Drain the gelatine sheets and squeeze to remove excess water. Stir the wet gelatine into the hot juice and keep stirring until it's dissolved. Then add the remaining orange juice and the grenadine. Pour the mix into 2 glasses or metal pudding moulds and leave to cool. Then chill for about 2–3hours until set.

While waiting for the jellies to set, segment the oranges. To do this you need to cut the peel from the top and bottom of the oranges. Then, with an orange placed cut end down, slice off the skin and pith in strips, curving the knife around the bulge in the orange. Then, holding the whole orange in your hand, carefully cut between the membranes to release the flesh segments.

If set in moulds, loosen the jelly by pulling it gently away from the top of the mould with your finger tips. Upend the mould on to a small flat dish and shake hard until you feel the jelly ease away and flop out. Serve the segments on the side. If serving in glasses simply pile the segments on top. Delicious when served chilled.

Cardamom and rose water rice pudding moulds

Indian sweets are very exciting – especially in their use of spices and gold leaf – edible gold, how glam and decadent is that! The set rice puddings are very low in fat, and still look beautiful at a dinner party. This dessert can also be made the day before, giving you plenty of time to yourself before the guests arrive.

Indian sweets are very exciting

Servings 4
Preparation Time 5 minutes, plus 1 hour to set
Cooking Time 20 minutes

750ml skimmed milk
3 cardamom pods
Small knob butter
225g pudding rice
50g fruit sugar, or 75g caster sugar
3 tbsp rose water
1 tbsp chopped pistachio nuts, to decorate
A handful fresh rose petals, to decorate
Edible gold leaf to decorate (optional)

Gently warm the milk in a medium saucepan until it reaches boiling point. Crush the cardamom pods. In a separate large non-stick saucepan, melt the butter and cook the rice and cardamom pods for about a minute, stirring until the rice becomes translucent. Slowly add the milk to the rice with a ladle, giving a few stirs and letting the rice absorb the liquid between each ladleful. The rice should take about 30–35 minutes to cook. It will be soft but should still have a bit of texture to the grains, like a risotto. Halfway through the cooking time, stir in the sugar.

When the rice is cooked and the liquid is almost absorbed, remove the saucepan from the heat. Discard the cardamom pods and add the rose water. Leave to cool a little. Line four individual pudding moulds, or ramekins, with clingfilm. Fill the moulds with the rice mix, patting down to ensure there are no trapped air bubbles. Cover with more clingfilm and chill until completely set, this should take about 1 hour.

To serve, turn the puddings out on to pretty plates. Sprinkle with pistachios and rose petals. You can also decorate the puddings with small scrunches of edible gold leaf.

Jasmine chocolate pots

Sometimes you need a true chocolate hit, when nothing but the good stuff will do. Well, here are my little scented pots of joy! These are satisfyingly rich, with a sneaky way of avoiding cream, so you won't need to over indulge, and they look rather classy. Pairing chocolate with unique flavours is very much in fashion now. I sometimes make this with a Mayan influence and add chilli and cinnamon instead of jasmine.

These are satisfyingly rich, with a sneaky way of avoiding cream

Serves 4
Preparation time   10 minutes,
                      plus setting time
Cooking time   10 minutes

250ml milk
2 tbsp jasmine tea leaves,
or green jasmine tea leaves
1 vanilla pod, split
50g icing sugar
150g dark chocolate, at least 60% cocoa solids
3 egg yolks

Heat the milk up to boiling point in a saucepan, then remove from the heat and stir in the tea leaves. Slit the vanilla pod lengthways and, using the tip of a sharp knife, scrape out the sticky seeds. Add these to the hot milk along with the pod and leave to infuse for 30 minutes.

Strain the milk through a sieve into a jug, then return the milk to the pan. Discard the tea leaves and vanilla pod. Reheat the milk and stir in the sugar until fully dissolved. Remove from the heat again and break in the chocolate, stirring until the chocolate has melted and the mixture is smooth. Beat in the egg yolks, one by one. Then pour the chocolate custard into four ramekins or small coffee cups. Leave to cool, then chill until set.

I serve these with biscotti (see page 66) but instead of making them with macadamia nuts and lemon, I might try them with almonds and mandarin oil (or orange zest).

PRE-PARTY STOMACH LINERS

I **love a good party** and also I'm quite partial to a good drink, but there is nothing worse than peaking too soon (if you know what I mean). Being drunk pre-dinner is something one should always try and avoid. I eat a little something before I go out and though you may think that this means you eat much more, in actual fact it lines your stomach and stops you from stuffing yourself at dinner. I hate being tired after a **HUGE** meal but with these recipes you'll be fit and ready for bouncing around the dance floor come twelve o'clock.

Don't be fooled into thinking that pre-party snacks gives you carte blanche to drink ten martinis, (which I only sometimes do . . . whoops!). You still need to **drink carefully**.

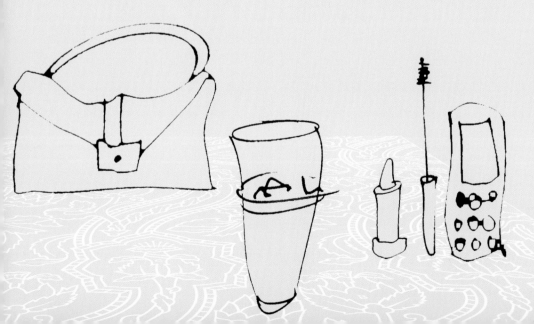

Mango, lime and coconut smoothie

I am not usually a smoothie girl (give me a glass of champagne any day) but this one is delicious, with lower fat coconut milk and sweet banana and mango. The lime gives it a little aromatic twist and brings the flavours together. This smoothie is great for breakfast too, or before you hit the gym . . . I know, *as if,* but the gym is a good idea occasionally, just leave the high heels at home!

The lime gives it a little aromatic twist and brings the flavours together

Serves 2
Preparation time   2 minutes

1 large juicy ripe mango (*very* important, no rock-hard tasteless mangoes here, please!)
1 large ripe banana
1 x 400ml can reduced-fat coconut milk
Juice 1 lime
1 tbsp palm sugar or muscovado sugar (optional)

This is so simple: just peel the mango and cut the flesh into rough cubes. Pop into a blender with the banana and blitz until smooth.

Pour in the coconut milk, add the lime juice and blitz again. Add the sugar, if you like, for that palm-sugar-like toffee flavour. Then gulp it down while you pop on your party frock!

Sourdough, avocado and sweet chilli crostinis

If you want a super-quick snack while running out the door, this hits the spot! Sourdough bread has a wonderful chewy texture and the avocado is like creamy butter. Avocadoes are such little gems – rich and satisfying and full of nature's good fats. I am a chilli addict, so a drizzle of sweet chilli sauce finishes this off perfectly. If you want to be super healthy, top with a squeeze of lemon juice, sea salt and freshly cracked black pepper.

Avocadoes are such little gems – rich and satisfying and full of nature's good fats

Makes 2
Preparation time   2 minutes

2 slices sourdough bread (Poilâne is my favourite and I sometimes use rye bread, but any good baker's bread would be just as delicious)
1 ripe avocado, halved and stoned
2 tsp of sweet chilli sauce
Sea salt

Toast or chargrill the bread. Meanwhile, scoop out the flesh from each half of the avocado with a large tablespoon, spoon on to the hot toast slices and mash with a fork to spread.

Sprinkle with some sea salt and drizzle with the chilli sauce. That's it! Yum yum.

Fried eggs with dates

When my favourite man in the world cooked me breakfast recently, this moreish dish reinforced my adoration! The dish is Persian in origin, and works very well with hot toast. Persian food is beautiful, full of complex flavours and layered textures.

Persian food is beautiful, full of complex flavours and layered textures

Serves 2
Preparation time   3 minutes
Cooking time   3 minutes

2 slices farmhouse-style bread (hopefully, it goes without saying that sliced white is not an option)
Small knob of butter
2 free-range organic eggs
4 large dates, ideally Iranian, stones removed and each cut in three large pieces

Put the bread on to toast. Heat the butter gently in a small omelette- or frying-pan. Crack in the eggs and sprinkle the dates into the whites. Cook until the white is completely set and the yolks runny. Sprinkle with a little salt to taste and serve.

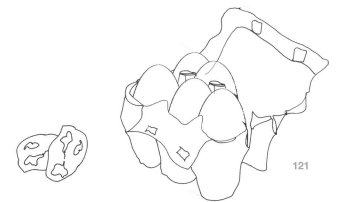

LOW CALORIE COCKTAILS

OK, so drinking is bad for you: check. Alcohol is full of empty calories: check. Being drunk is particularly unhealthy (and un-glam): check.

We all know the dangers of drinking, yet somehow forget it when heading to the bar. I can't work miracles but there are certainly some drinks that are slightly better than others, both for your waistline and your poor head the next morning.

These are the drinks to avoid:

BEER: Why the HELL would you drink this stuff anyway? Leave it to the boys: beer tastes awful, bloats your stomach and comes in unsightly big glasses. Just say no! Beer is only acceptable if travelling through a hot country with a hot guy, and even then as a rare indulgence.

ALCOPOPS: Sorry, how old did you say you were? Are you even old enough to buy this book? These are the worst offenders of all. They come in luminous colours, are full of sugars and nasty chemicals and are possibly best suited to being used as loo cleaner.

DARK SPIRITS: While they can seem quite sophisticated, dark spirits pack a punch in the calories department and have a strong alcoholic hit, so just be careful.

COCKTAILS: I love cocktails, but you need to think sexy martinis instead of sex on the beach. Any with dodgy names are usually best avoided, unless you are trying to pull the barman and are using them as some sort of innuendo. Whatever floats your boat…or, in fact, whatever works! Also avoid all creamy ones.

These are the lesser offenders:

CHAMPAGNE: There are a million reasons why champagne is the best. I do love champagne, it makes you feel happy and special (in moderation) and it's lower in calories than most other drinks. Ultra Brut Champagne is fantastic, but very dry. All the models love it.

WHITE WINE: The drier the better here, no pudding wines. White wine spritzers are especially good.

PALE SPIRITS: I am by no means recommending knocking back the voddy on a regular basis, but combined with a low-sugar mixer (like soda water, not the artificially sweetened stuff) and finished with a big squeeze of lime, it's not as bad as others.

Here are some of my favourite concoctions that avoid the nasties and are still delicious, so enjoy . . . but not too much!

Wasabi bloody Marys

Bloody Marys are my partners in crime on a Sunday morning. As a hangover cure they're tough to beat but I think the wasabi makes a fun change to surprise people with. Be warned though, wasabi is extremely hot so use too much and people will really get a surprise!

My partner in crime on a Sunday morning

Serves 6
Preparation time 5 minutes

1 litre V8 vegetable juice or tomato juice, well chilled
200ml good-quality vodka, chilled
1 tbsp Worcestershire sauce
Juice 1 lemon
1–3 tsp wasabi paste, according to taste

Just mix all the ingredients together in a large jug, and serve poured over ice cubes!

Turn to page 82 for another recipe using wasabi

Elderflower and apple Bellinis

Bellinis are a lovely start to a meal and these are fresh-tasting and elegant. They are also super simple to make and rather English, so would go down a treat with an afternoon tea.

They are also super simple to make and rather English

Makes 4
Preparation time   5 minutes

20ml elderflower cordial
40ml cloudy apple juice
Roughly 600ml prosecco, cava or champagne
4 champagne glasses

Basically, just divide the cordial between each glass, then add the apple juice and finally top up with the bubbly. Enjoy!

Mandarin Caprioskas

Lime- and vodka-laced Caprioskas are my favourite cocktails, though they are very strong so need to be sipped in a lady-like fashion! Here I have replaced the limes with mandarins. If you want to up the flavour, add a little splash of Cointreau too.

They are very strong so need to be sipped in a lady-like fashion!

Makes 1 glass
Preparation time 5 minutes

1 mandarin or clementine
2 tsp light muscovado sugar
2 shots vodka
Soda water to top up

Cut the mandarin into small chunks (skin and flesh), pop into a short tumbler and then stir in the sugar. Take a small rolling pin or thick wooden spoon and crush the mandarins and sugar together. Add crushed ice and top up with soda water.

For another calorie-conscious drink, have a vodka and soda in normal measures and squeeze in two lime wedges.

Lemongrass, chilli and kaffir lime leaf Collins

This is a long and refreshing cocktail. It's good for balmy summer evenings and has a little chilli-infused bite to it.

Makes about 6
Preparation time   5 minutes

For the syrup
2 sticks lemongrass
1 large red fresh chilli
3 kaffir lime leaves, ideally fresh but dried is fine
100g fruit sugar

For each glass
1 tbsp syrup above
1 part gin
½ lime
Crushed ice
4 parts soda water

Cut the lemongrass sticks in half and bash the stems with a rolling pin. Cut the chilli in half and scrunch up the lime leaves. Pop the lemongrass, chilli and lime leaves into a saucepan with the sugar and 250ml of water. Bring to the boil, turn down and simmer gently for 10 minutes until reduced by half. Take off the heat and leave to cool. When ready to serve, strain the syrup into a small jug and discard the aromatics.

Pour about a tablespoon of the syrup into a tall glass and a shot of gin (about 30ml – roughly an eggcup). Cut the lime into quarters, squeeze the juice into the glass and drop the wedge in also. Add a handful of crushed ice and top up with about four parts soda water.

Basil and white peach Bellinis

The Bellini was invented in the Venice Cipriani hotel. It is a true classic and hard to beat. My basil and peach version will add sparkle to any dinner party . . .

Makes about 6
Preparation time   10 minutes

2 white peaches, halved and roughly chopped
Small bunch fresh basil, about 25g
1 75cl bottle prosecco or dry sparkling white wine, chilled

Blitz the peach and basil together in a food processor. Rub the mixture through a sieve with a wooden spoon or the back of a ladle. Pour into 6 tall champagne flutes and top with prosecco.

HEARTY HEALTHY HANGOVER CURES

You obviously haven't read the last few pages, have you? **Naughty girl!** Mind you, with all the good will in the world, killer hangovers can come out of nowhere.

I can have a civilised two glasses of vino one night and feel rotten the next day, and in turn can be knocking back martinis like James Bond another night and feel fine the next morning. It doesn't make sense!

Anyway, you don't need me nagging you today – **time for serious hangover cures!** I'm not going to start recommending 'hair of the dog' or knocking back raw eggs, but what you do need is good nutrition for your seriously depleted body.

People often resort to the quick fix of greasy or stodgy food when hung-over but don't do it. It will just make you feel worse and also lead to spots and piling on the pounds. **Fast food should be avoided at all costs.** The right kinds of fat in the right quantities won't hurt though, and right now it's all about feeling better!

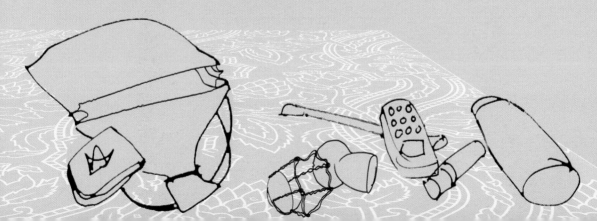

My comforting kedgeree

Kedgeree is a classic and one of the best dishes to serve for brunch. It's wonderfully comforting to see the mounds of beautifully spiced rice, pale yellow flakes of haddock, and boiled eggs. I sometimes serve it with poached eggs, so the egg yolk mingles with the rice, but that depends on how much time I have!

A classic and one of the best dishes to serve for brunch

Serves 2
Preparation time   10 minutes
Cooking time   20 minutes

250g un-dyed smoked haddock fillet
200ml milk
2 bay leaves (optional)
½ small onion, roughly chopped (optional)
2 free-range organic eggs
25g butter
2 tsp olive oil
6 spring onions, sliced
2 garlic cloves, chopped
300–400g cooked basmati rice (or cook 125–150g raw rice according to packet instructions)
2 tsp curry powder
2 tsp mango chutney
Small handful fresh coriander leaves
Lemon wedges, to serve
Sea salt and freshly ground black pepper, plus some peppercorns for poaching

Place the haddock in a deep frying pan and cover with milk. Add a bay leaf, a few peppercorns and the roughly sliced onion, if using. Gently bring to the boil, and then take off the heat and leave to cool. Discard the bay leaf and onion.

At the same time put the eggs (in their shells) into a pan of cold water, bring to the boil and simmer for 6 minutes. Remove from the heat and cool under cold running water. These should be slightly soft in the centre but if you prefer them harder then cook for a further 2 minutes.

When the fish is cool enough to handle, lift the haddock out of the milk with a fish slice and lay on a plate. Peel off the skin and roughly flake the flesh, removing any bones. Keep the flakes of haddock as large as possible as they will break up when mixed into the rice.

Heat a wok or large frying pan and add the butter, oil, spring onions and garlic. Fry for 2 minutes then add the curry powder and the rice. Stir for about 2–3 minutes until all the grains are piping hot and covered with the spicy butter. Fork in the mango chutney, haddock, coriander and seasoning then cook for a further 2 minutes until very hot. Peel and halve the eggs, which should still be a little runny. Pile the fishy rice on two plates, top with the egg halves and serve with a wedge of lemon.

Pan-fried chorizo, cherry tomatoes and chillies on toast

This is something I eat often when I'm hung-over, (sometimes missing out the chorizo when I feel so bad that even walking to the local shop is too much). It has the same sort of flavours as a Bloody Mary, which people drink to get back on form after a heavy night. The reason Bloody Marys are so popular is due to the lycopene (an antioxidant) in tomatoes. Lycopene is stronger in cooked tomatoes, so this dish is a blinder. The chilli and garlic have cleansing effects which wake you up, and the fat from the chorizo lets your body know that you're full. After this you'll be back on your feet in no time!

The chilli and garlic have cleansing effects which wake you up

Serves 2
Preparation time   5 minutes
Cooking time   12 minutes

50g small chorizo sausages, sliced
2 garlic cloves, sliced
300g cherry tomatoes, halved (you can use canned tomatoes, especially if you're feeling too sick to get to the shops!)
1 tsp olive oil
Pinch dried chillies
1–2 tsp Worcestershire sauce (optional)
2 tsp reduced-fat crème fraîche
Small handful basil leaves
Small handful coriander leaves
Pinch sugar
Sea salt, freshly ground black pepper
2 slices good bread (I love using black-olive ciabatta or Poilâne sourdough. I also sometimes make my own green olive bread, but you're hung-over so sod that!)

Slice the chorizo and garlic and halve the cherry tomatoes. Heat the olive oil in a frying pan. Fry the chorizo for about 2 minutes, until the fat comes out and the slices start to crisp. Then add the garlic and chilli. Continue frying for a further 2–3 minutes, taking care not to burn the chorizo.

Add the tomatoes and Worcestershire sauce (if using) and check the seasoning. Turn the heat down as the tomatoes soften and give off their juice. Simmer for about 5 minutes then add the crème fraîche and herbs.

If I have the energy, I chargrill the bread but you can just pop it in the toaster. Pile each toasted slice with the chorizo and tomato mix and chow down. Then drink a large glass of water and go back to sleep!

Turn to pages 168–9 for another recipe using chorizo

Chive French toast with smoked salmon and ricotta

This is a very quick and satisfying breakfast, yet it has a sophisticated vibe to it, too. It's more a *Sex and the City* brunch than 'a hangover and the sofa' meal. Knock this up and you'll be skipping down the street like Carrie Bradshaw by the afternoon!

A very quick and satisfying breakfast

Serves 2
Preparation time   5 minutes
Cooking time   8 minutes

2 free-range eggs
3 tbsp milk
2 tbsp fresh chives, chopped
1 tbsp fresh tarragon leaves, chopped
2 slices seeded bread (Burgen bread is good)
2 tbsp olive oil
2 tbsp reduced-fat ricotta (look for 9% fat)
100g smoked salmon
Grated zest 1 lemon
Sea salt and freshly ground black pepper

Beat together the eggs, milk, herbs and seasoning. Dip both sides of each bread slice into the egg mix so they are well coated, then place on a plate.

Heat the olive oil in a large non-stick pan and then carefully lay in the bread slices. Cook for a few minutes on each side until golden brown.

Spread the ricotta on the toast and serve with the smoked salmon twisted attractively on top. Sprinkle with the lemon zest and freshly ground black pepper to serve.

 Turn to page 110–1 for another recipe using ricotta

Masala eggs with cooling coriander yogurt

The everyday food eaten in India is nothing like the high-fat oily dishes we call Indian cuisine in Britain. I ate this wonderfully spiced omelette and wholemeal chapattis in India a few years ago. The spices really wake you up and the chapattis are great to wrap the eggs up in. My take on the dish is made with eggs and peppers.

The spices really wake you up

Serves 2
Preparation time   15 minutes
Cooking time   15 minutes

1 red pepper, quartered, deseeded and sliced
1 green pepper, quartered, deseeded and sliced
1 large fresh red chilli, slit, deseeded and chopped
1 garlic clove, chopped
1 red onion, chopped
2 tbsp olive oil
2 tsp garam masala or medium curry powder
4 free-range eggs
Wholemeal chapattis, to serve
Sea salt and freshly ground black pepper

For the tomato relish

3 ripe tomatoes
½ red onion
¼ cucumber
Juice ½ lemon

For the coriander yogurt

½ bunch coriander (about 10g, including the stalks)
About 5 stems fresh mint
150g bio live yogurt

To make the relish, chop the tomatoes, cucumber and onion into small, similar-sized pieces and mix with the lemon juice. Set this mix to one side. Then make the yogurt dip by popping all the ingredients into a blender and blitzing until fine. Chill the yogurt mix in the fridge.

Heat up a large frying pan and add the olive oil. Stir in the prepared peppers, onion, chilli and garlic. Fry on a medium heat for about 5 minutes and add the garam masala, then continue cooking for a further 5 minutes until softened.

Make four wells in the pepper mix and crack an egg into each hole. Season the tops of the eggs and continue cooking until they are cooked to your liking. Sometimes I pop the pan under a hot grill for a few minutes to set the tops.

Divide the eggs and vegetables on to two warmed plates. Serve with the yogurt and relish alongside and the wholemeal chapattis to dunk into the eggs.

 Turn to pages 64–5 and 192 for more recipes using yogurt

Superfood burger

Hangover equals burger for me, but if I ever succumb to fast food I always regret it. Not only is fast food greasy and unsatisfying, you know that it's also doing you harm and it tastes HORRIBLE. So I thought up this superfood burger! It's made up of nutrient-rich foods to make you feel good, and is a world away from nasty fast food.

A world away from nasty fast food

Serves 2
Preparation time   15 minutes
Cooking time   20 minutes

1 red onion
1 medium sweet potato
2 tbsp olive oil
1 small ripe avocado
2 tsp lemon juice
25g soft blue cheese
250g turkey mince
½ 200g can sweetcorn, drained
1 clove garlic, crushed
Pinch chilli powder
2 tbsp fresh coriander, chopped
1 free-range egg yolk
1 beef tomato, sliced
4 slices cooked beetroot
Sea salt and freshly ground black pepper

First, preheat the oven to 200°C, Gas Mark 6. Slice the onion and sweet potato into 1cm-thick slices. Lay the slices on a tray, drizzle with the olive oil and season with salt and pepper. Roast for about 20 minutes until just tender. Remove and leave to cool.

While the onion and sweet potatoes are cooking, peel and mash the avocado, lemon juice and blue cheese together. Set to one side.

Mix together the turkey mince, sweetcorn, garlic, chilli, coriander, egg yolk and seasoning. Shape the mix into 2 burgers. Heat a ridged griddle pan or heavy non-stick frying pan and cook for about 5 minutes on each side over a medium heat until firm when pressed lightly. Remove and leave to stand for 5 minutes.

To serve, divide the sweet potato between two plates. Lay the slices of tomato on top, then the burger, beetroot and finally a dollop of the mashed avocado. Serve and enjoy!

Mexican beans

This is a slight cheat and though I don't advocate processed canned foods, this is for times of need! It is always better to make something at home, and avoid pizza on speed dial, even when desperate for an emergency hangover cure.

This is for times of need!

Serves 2
Preparation time 5 minutes
Cooking time   10 minutes

150g can baked beans
½ tsp smoked paprika
½ tsp ground cumin
½ tsp ground coriander
½ tsp cayenne
2 slices wholemeal bread
4 free-range eggs
Splash milk
25g Cheddar cheese, grated
1 tbsp olive oil
1–2 tsp sliced pickled jalapeño peppers, to garnish (optional)
Sea salt and freshly ground black pepper

Mix together the beans and spices in a saucepan and heat gently until bubbling. Put the bread on to toast.

To make the scrambled eggs, whisk the eggs, milk and cheese in a bowl. Heat the olive oil in a medium-size non-stick saucepan then pour in the egg mixture. Stir continuously for about 4–6 minutes until cooked and creamy. Check the seasoning.

Pour the beans first on to the toast, then top with the eggs and serve garnished with the peppers, if liked.

Turn to page 27 for another recipe using jalapeño peppers

BRUNCH IDEAS

Brunch isn't as big in the UK as it is in America and Australia where they do it so well. **I am a huge fan of brunch** and all of these recipes work well for a hangover, too.

There is something so lovely about piles of newspapers, feel-good music and great company, all enjoyed over a delightful brunch. It kind of makes your toes curl in pleasure! These are my transatlantic brunch ideas; I hope you're going to **invite me round!**

Brown sugar- and Pernod-cured salmon with fennel shavings and homemade soda bread

The concept of curing salmon sounds very time-consuming and a wee bit too housewifely. But don't worry, I haven't lost all my sense and sensibility, this dish is very simple and your guests will think you are a culinary princess. Which of course you are!

The soda bread is so quick, it's a wonder that we don't make it every morning. It's at its best when warm so, as the chef has special privileges, sneak yourself a little slice . . .

Serves 4
Preparation time   30 minutes, plus 8–12 hours marinating time
Cooking time   40 minutes

1 small side of salmon, about 400g
200g sea salt
250g brown sugar, such as demerara
Grated zest two lemons and juice of one
2 tbsp Pernod or ouzo
2 heads fennel (reserve the leafy fronds)
2 tbsp olive oil
Small bunch chives, sliced thinly
200ml reduced-fat crème fraîche
1 lemon, cut in wedges, to serve
Sea salt and freshly ground white pepper

For the soda bread
250g plain flour
250g wholemeal flour
1 tsp bicarbonate of soda
1 tsp sea salt
1 tsp fruit sugar
450ml buttermilk (or a mix of half natural-yogurt and half skimmed-milk)

You'll need to prepare the fish the day before you want to serve this dish. First, check the fish for any stray bones and pull them out. Trim the side of salmon to neaten and lay in a large flat dish. Mix the salt, sugar and lemon zest together. Pat this mix all over the flesh side of the fish and then sprinkle over the Pernod.

Cover the fish with clingfilm and lay a chopping board directly on top of the fish. Place the dish in the fridge and pop something else heavy on top, like a few cans of beans or a bag of potatoes, to press down the salmon. Leave it for at least 8 hours, though if you have time 12 hours is ideal.

Make the bread the following morning. Preheat the oven to 200°C, Gas Mark 6. Stir all the dry ingredients together in a large mixing bowl. Make a well in the centre and pour in the buttermilk. Gradually mix to make a dough but do not overbeat as this will make it tough. In fact, don't mess around too much with it at all!

Shape into a large round on a non-stick baking sheet (or one lined with baking parchment) and cut a large cross on the top. Bake for about 40 minutes. You can test it's done by turning it upside down and tapping the bottom: it should sound hollow.

While the bread is cooking, make the salad. Finely slice the fennel on a mandolin or Japanese food slicer (or simply use a very sharp thin-bladed knife) and mix with the lemon juice, 2 tbsp of olive oil and seasoning.

Take the salmon out of the fridge. Wash the salt and sugar mix off the salmon and pat dry. Finely chop the fennel fronds. Sprinkle them over the salmon and press into the flesh. Then slice the salmon on a diagonal as thinly as possible, with a long sharp knife.

Arrange the salmon on a platter and pile the fennel salad in the centre. Mix the chives with the crème fraîche and serve alongside the salmon with the lemon wedges and chunks of warm soda bread.

Banana and macadamia bread with blueberries

I used to make this for breakfast when I lived in Australia. What a wonderful wake up, especially when paired with the white cockatoos calling and the smell of gum trees. It's moist and cake-like and a great way to start the day (although not the healthiest, as it does contain sugar). The macadamia nuts add a lovely waxy texture to the bread – a pure slice of happiness!

A pure slice of happiness!

Serves 8
Preparation time 15 minutes, plus cooling time
Cooking time 40 minutes

2 very ripe bananas
100g butter, melted
3 tbsp milk
1 free-range egg
50g macadamia nuts, chopped
250g plain flour
½ tsp bicarbonate of soda
¼ tsp baking powder
100g caster sugar
¼ tsp salt

To serve
150g 0% fat Greek yogurt
150g blueberries

Preheat the oven to 180°C, Gas Mark 4. Grease and line the base of a 500g loaf tin with a strip of baking parchment.

Pop the bananas into a blender with the butter, milk and egg and whiz until smooth and creamy. In a big bowl, mix the flour with the bicarbonate of soda, baking powder, sugar and salt, then stir in the nuts. Add the banana mixture and combine well.

Pour into the prepared tin. Bang the tin a few times on the worktop to level out the mixture. Bake for about 40 minutes until golden, risen and firm when pressed. Check the centre is cooked with a thin metal skewer – when slid into the centre of the cake it should come out clean.

Leave to cool in the tin for 15 minutes then turn out on to a wire rack. To serve, mix together the yogurt and blueberries. Slice the banana bread while still slightly warm and serve topped with the fruity yogurt.

If by some strange chain of events the banana bread doesn't get hoovered up in one brunch I chargrill it and serve it the next day too.

Turn to page 67 for another recipe using bananas

Salt cod brandade eggs Benedict

Salt cod features in lots of different cuisines, under many different names like Bacalao, Baccalà, Bacalhau and Morue. The French make it into a paste with garlic and herbs and call it brandade, which works really well with potatoes and eggs. I wanted to make something a little bit different from the usual eggs Benedict and this is it! If you can't find salt cod and don't fancy the salting process, then natural smoked haddock is also a dream in this dish.

A little bit different from the usual eggs Benedict

Serves 4
Preparation time 20 minutes, plus time for salting in the fridge
Cooking time 40 minutes

400g skinless cod fillet
100g sea salt
2 cloves garlic
2 sprigs thyme
500ml milk
500g waxy new potatoes
6 spring onions, thinly sliced
Handful sorrel leaves or flat-leaf parsley, chopped
1 tbsp olive oil
Good squeeze lemon juice
4 free-range eggs
Sea salt and freshly ground black pepper

For the hollandaise sauce
2 tbsp reduced-fat crème fraîche
2 tsp white wine vinegar
2 egg yolks
100g warm clarified butter (see below for my method)

Place the cod in a shallow dish and sprinkle the salt over the fish. Cover with clingfilm, chill in the fridge and leave for a minimum of 2 hours but up to 8 hours if you have the time. Then rinse the salt off in cold running water and pat the cod dry.

Put the cod, garlic and thyme sprigs in a saucepan and cover with milk. Bring to the boil then simmer on a low heat for 10 minutes. Remove from the heat and leave the fish to cool in the milk.

Put the potatoes in a saucepan and cover with boiling water. Simmer for about 20 minutes until tender. I like to peel the potatoes for this dish *after* cooking, using rubber gloves to protect my hands from the heat but it's time-consuming and you do lose the nutrients from the skin – so it's your call. When the potatoes are cool enough to handle, crush them with your hands into a saucepan, or press against the side of a pan with a fork.

Drain the milk from the cod and garlic. In a bowl, mash the cod and garlic together with a fork, making sure they are well combined. Then mix in the potatoes, spring onions, sorrel or parsley. This makes the brandade. If you want the mixture to be a little softer then add a little of the milk. Check the seasoning – it might need pepper but not much salt. Then add the olive oil and a squeeze of lemon. Set aside and keep warm.

To make the hollandaise, first beat the crème fraîche until it thickens. Set it to one side. Place the egg yolks into a large heatproof bowl that will fit snugly over a saucepan of gently simmering water. Add the vinegar to the yolks and 2 good

pinches of salt. Using an electric whisk, beat until very light and fluffy, being careful not to overheat the bowl as the eggs will scramble. Remove the bowl from the pan if it starts to get too hot. The egg yolks should not cook, just thicken.

With the bowl back on the heat, slowly trickle in the butter, whisking as you pour so the butter is emulsified. Take care not to add too much butter at once or the mixture might separate. When the mixture is pale, gradually add the butter in a small steady stream as you continue to whisk. Wait until it thickens before you add more butter. Remove the bowl from the heat and whisk in the crème fraîche to lighten it. Add lemon juice to taste and check the seasoning. Keep the hollandaise warm on the edge of the stove and don't let it get cold or set.

To poach the eggs, heat a frying pan of water, add another tsp of vinegar and bring to the boil. Turn the heat to a simmer and crack in the eggs one at a time. Cook for 2–3 minutes until the yolks are just set but still a little runny. Lift the eggs out with a fish slice and drain on a paper towel.

Spoon the brandade into the centre of warmed plates, top with the eggs and drizzle over a small amount of the hollandaise – you won't need to use it all. Grind some pepper over the dish and serve.

How I clarify butter

Heat 125g unsalted butter in a pan and melt (or do this in a microwave). When melted, leave to stand for a minute then carefully pour off the golden oil. Discard the milky juices left behind.

Feta hotcakes with honey and crispy bacon

I have a confession: I *love* pancakes! Unfortunately they're not the best breakfast for me as I get a sugar-rush high followed by a bad mood during the comedown . . . we call it pancake rage. But these healthy alternatives have just a drizzle of honey so you don't need to worry about sugar-rush fall-out! The buckwheat flour is a fantastic, healthy alternative to wheat with its slow energy-releasing carbohydrates. The combination of feta and bacon will really get your taste buds going in the a.m.

The combination of feta and bacon will really get your taste buds going

Serve 4
Preparation time 15 minutes,
plus resting time
Cooking time 15 minutes

150g buckwheat flour (which can be bought from good health food stores)
50g wholemeal flour
1 tsp bicarbonate of soda
1 free-range egg
500ml skimmed milk
100g reduced-fat feta, crumbled
8 slices streaky smoked bacon
Corn oil for cooking
2–4 tbsp runny honey

Mix all the dry ingredients together in a large bowl and make a well in the centre with a wooden spoon. Whisk the egg and milk together, pour into the well and beat, gradually drawing the flour into the centre until you have a smooth batter. Crumble in the feta and set aside to rest for 10 minutes.

Heat the grill to a high temperature and grill the bacon until really crispy. Drain on a paper towel while you make the hotcakes.

Heat a heavy-based frying pan until hot and add a teaspoon or two of corn oil. Using a medium ladle, spoon batter into the pan. One ladleful will make 2–3 hotcakes. If you don't have a ladle, then use about 2 tbsps. Cook the hotcakes for about 2 minutes until bubbles start to appear on the surface, then flip them over and cook for another minute. The hotcakes should be nicely golden brown.

Repeat until all the batter has been used. You should make at least 12 hotcakes, making 3 per person. Top each serving with 2 rashers of bacon and drizzle over some honey to serve.

Turn to pages 38–9, 73 and 102 for more recipes using feta

Spiced poached apricots and figs

Cardamom is often used in Indian desserts, and I think using the spice with these apricots is a different and tasty pudding option. You can use lots of varieties of fruit too, so experiment. Poached fruit is a wonderfully colourful way to start the day, especially with a dollop of Greek yogurt.

Poached fruit is a wonderfully colourful way to start the day

Serves 4
Preparation time   5 minutes
Cooking time   15 minutes

300g fresh apricots
300g fresh figs, deep purple ones if possible
150g fruit sugar
3 cardamom pods
1 stick cinnamon
2 tsp orange-flower water
Juice ½ lemon

I like the fruit in this recipe to stay whole so I just clean the apricots and figs and then trim a little off the fig stalks.

Put the sugar, spices and 700ml of water into a pan and bring to the boil. Add the fruit and simmer gently for about 5 minutes until the apricots and figs are tender but keep their shape.

Take the fruit out of the water with a slotted spoon and continue to boil the syrup until reduced down by half (or until it's glossy and thick). Stir in the orange-flower water and lemon juice and remove from the heat.

Return the fruit to the syrup and leave to chill. The dish is then ready to be served with yogurt or toasted brioche.

Turn to pages 160–1 and 166 for more recipes using figs

AFTERNOON TEA DELIGHTS

Marie-Antoinette had the right idea when she said, '**Let them eat cake.**' I love afternoon tea. In France, when served with champagne it is called *le goûter* (the taster). Let's face it, the French do it better, so I'm inclined to go for a French-style tea, though when it comes to the cuppa itself the Brits rule and there is nothing like a cup of Earl Grey or Rose Pouchong. It's your call, and it can be **as dressy or as casual as you please.**

So bring on the scented flowers, mismatched crockery, old lace tablecloths and **get nibbling on pretty cakes**. It's just like the old days! A tea like this can be so pretty and so fun. I organised an especially whimsical afternoon tea as a baby shower for a famous client of mine and everyone adored it.

Passion-fruit jellies with white chocolate cream and ginger shortbreads

Jellies are wonderful as they don't contain fat and are a good way to get some extra fruit into your day! Passion fruit is a great flavour and works well in this dish. These are extremely pretty little puds, accompanied by the white chocolate and shortbreads. If you want to be more healthy, miss out the chocolate and biscuit and top with passion fruit seeds instead.

Makes 20

Preparation time   45 minutes, plus setting time and 30 minutes for chilling

Cooking time   30 minutes

8 leaves gelatine
800ml passion fruit-flavoured juice, such as a tropical fruit juice
8–10 ripe passion fruits
200g white chocolate
250ml reduced-fat crème fraîche

For the shortbreads
150g plain flour
75g fruit sugar
1 tbsp chopped stem ginger
125g chilled butter

First, make the jellies. Soak the gelatine in a large bowl of cold water until floppy then drain and gently squeeze out excess water. Gently heat 150ml of the fruit juice until very hot and just below boiling point. Remove from the heat and stir in the gelatine until dissolved. Then add the rest of the juice. Leave to cool and then chill lightly until it begins to set. Put 20 shot glasses out on a tray that will fit on your fridge shelf.

Halve four or five of the passion fruits and divide the pulp between the shot glasses. Pour the chilled, almost-setting jelly into the glasses – leave enough space to add a spoonful of the white chocolate cream later. Place the tray in the fridge overnight or until fully set.

To make the shortbreads, preheat the oven to 150°C Gas Mark 2. Mix together the flour, sugar and ginger. Cut the butter into small cubes and mix into the flour. Then, using an electric mixer (ideally with a dough hook if you have one), mix to a dough. If you don't have an electric mixer, rub the butter and dry ingredients together with your hands until the dough comes together. Make sure not to over-knead.

On a lightly floured board, roll the dough into a sausage about 3cm wide. Wrap the roll in clingfilm and chill for about for 30 minutes. Line a baking sheet with baking parchment.

Using a sharp knife, cut the dough roll into 5mm slices. Lay each slice on the baking sheet and bake for 20 minutes until pale golden, but not too coloured. You should check the slices halfway through, turning the baking sheet around if necessary. Slide the biscuits on to a wire rack and leave to cool.

Meanwhile, make the white chocolate cream. Break the chocolate into a heatproof bowl and melt either on a low heat in a microwave for 3–5 minutes or over a pan of very gently simmering water. Remove from the heat, stir gently and mix in the crème fraîche. Remove and leave to cool for about 20 minutes, stirring once or twice. Spoon on to the jellies. Halve the remaining passion fruits and spoon the pulp over the peaks of chocolate cream. Serve with a little round of shortbread balanced on the edge of each glass.

Little angel cakes

These are almost fat-free cakes but before the stampede begins, ladies, just be warned this doesn't mean you get to eat thirty but it does mean they are better for you than your average muffin. These angels would also make Marie Antoinette proud with their cuteness: I love having fun with the decorating, and kids love making these too!

These angels would make Marie Antoinette proud with their cuteness

Makes 25–30
Preparation time   30 minutes, plus time for
                       icing and decoration
Cooking time   12 minutes

Up to 30 mini-muffin cases, silver and gold
2 free-range eggs, separated
125g fruit sugar, or 180g caster sugar
1 tsp vanilla extract
150g self-raising flour
1 tsp sea salt

For decoration
250g Royal icing sugar, sifted (and water to add)
2–3 food colourings
Coloured sparkles, (dragées) to sprinkle on top

Line two mini-muffin tins with the paper cases. Heat the oven to 180°C, Gas Mark 4. Whip the egg yolks, half the sugar and the vanilla together in a large bowl until pale and fluffy. Sift together the flour and salt and fold into the egg mix with a large metal spoon.

In a large, very clean bowl whisk the egg whites until they form soft peaks, then gradually whisk in the remaining sugar until it becomes glossy. Fold the egg whites and sugar into the main mix. Spoon into the little muffin cases.

Bake for 10–12 minutes until the angel cakes have risen and are firm when pressed on top. Remove and leave to cool on a wire rack.

Meanwhile, sift the icing sugar into a big bowl and gradually beat in tepid water according to pack instructions, to a pouring consistency. Divide the icing into two or three batches. Carefully add tiny drops of colouring to the different batches. I usually choose duck-egg blue, pale pink, pistachio green and pale yellow. Spoon a small amount of coloured icing on to each cake. Then add contrasting coloured sprinkles, if you like. Allow the icing to set and then serve.

Salted chocolate caramel éclairs

The fashion for salted caramel chocolates has been around for a while but it's still surprising what an amazing new taste dimension the sea salt crystals add. I can't say that any of the little titbits in this section are 100 per cent healthy, as sugar just isn't good for you. But I have tried to limit the damage: the filling in these éclairs is normally made with cream and egg yolks whereas I've used skimmed milk and fruit sugar. Making little changes, without compromising on flavour, is the way to drop the calories!

Makes about 20–24
Preparation time   40 minutes
Cooking time   50–55 minutes

50g butter, cut in small cubes
100g plain flour, sifted, with a pinch of salt
2 large free-range eggs, beaten
150g good quality milk chocolate (or dark if you want to reduce the sugar content)
A little Maldon sea salt flakes (or I use pink Murray River sea salt crystals from Australia)

For the filling
1 vanilla pod
250ml skimmed milk
40g fruit sugar or 60g caster sugar
50g cornflour

Make the filling first. Split the vanilla pod in half lengthways and, using the tip of a sharp knife, scrape the seeds into a medium saucepan with the milk. Heat gently until hot and then set aside.

In a separate heavy-based saucepan, combine the sugar and 2 tablespoons of cold water. Swirl, but don't stir, as the water is absorbed by the sugar. Allow to stand for 5 minutes to saturate then place over a low heat. Continue to heat without stirring for about 5 minutes and the crystals will begin to dissolve. Try not to get the sugar crystals up the sides of the pan or the syrup might begin to crystallise. When the sugar becomes a clear syrup, turn up the heat and bring to the boil. Continue to boil for about 3–5 minutes, still without stirring, until a medium-dark caramel forms. Remove from the heat.

Be SUPER careful now – this stuff is very hot and will take your skin off if it makes contact. Don't take your eyes off the pan for a second. Carefully pour the milk into the caramel, stirring with a long-handled wooden spoon until smooth. It will splutter and spit but do continue to stir and it will calm down.

Mix the cornflour with a tablespoon or two of cold water to make a smooth paste. Place the caramel milk back on the heat and stir in the cornflour mix. Reheat until thickened and bubbling and then pour into a bowl and leave to cool, stirring once or twice to prevent a skin forming. Cover with clingfilm and set aside.

To make the choux pastry, place 200ml of cold water into a medium saucepan, add the butter and heat until the butter

melts. Turn up the heat until bubbling then immediately tip in the plain flour and stir briskly with a wooden spoon until the mixture becomes a smooth thick paste that comes away from the sides of the pan. It looks awful at first, but will magically come together. Continue to heat for another minute then remove the pan from the heat and leave to cool for 5 minutes.

Gradually beat in the eggs a third at a time until the paste loosens to a dropping consistency – when you lift up some of the mixture with the spoon, it will drop off when you shake the spoon sharply).

Heat the oven to 200°C, Gas Mark 6. Line a baking sheet with baking parchment. To make the éclairs, spoon the mixture into a large piping bag with a plain nozzle about 1cm diameter. Pipe 3cm lengths of the choux pastry mix along the sheet, spaced out to allow for expansion. You should get about 20–24 éclairs. Bake for about 15 minutes until puffed, crisp and golden brown. Don't take them out too soon, as they may deflate. Remove to a wire rack and, using the end of a teaspoon, make a small deep hole to allow the hot air to escape. Leave until quite cool.

Wash and dry the piping bag and nozzle and then fill the bag with the caramel filling. Push the nozzle into the small holes you made earlier with a teaspoon and pipe in the filling. Then pop them back on to the sheet.

Break up the chocolate and place in a heatproof bowl. Melt in a microwave on a medium heat for 2–3 minutes, stirring now and again, or place the bowl over a pan of gently simmering water. One by one, take each éclair, turn it upside down and dip the top in the chocolate. Place chocolate-side up on the baking sheet and crush over pinches of salt flakes. Allow to set – chill slightly if you want – then serve.

If you don't have a piping bag, or don't know how to pipe, then simply spoon heaped teaspoons of the choux pastry mix on to the baking paper, spaced out to allow for expansion. It doesn't matter if the blobs are a bit craggy, they even out when cooking. Bake for 15 minutes. As they cool, slit open. When cold, spoon the filling in and close up.

Making little changes, without compromising on flavour, is the way to drop the calories!

Pavlova with lemon fromage frais and blueberries

Pavlovas are a great centrepiece to a full afternoon tea. When you have one big dish, like a pavlova, I recommend making lots of little dainty treats too, to dot around for contrast.

Lemon and meringue is a long-standing marriage made in heaven, something that you have to respect. This is a lovely combination of flavours and textures, and looks absolutely stunning. My healthier recipe has a great alternative to the usual creamy filling, so get stuck in!

Lemon and meringue is a long-standing marriage made in heaven

Serves 4
Preparation time 20 minutes
Cooking time 1 hour

4 large free-range egg whites
Pinch salt
200g caster sugar
1 tsp cornflour
1 tsp lemon juice
500g tub reduced-fat fromage frais or
0% fat Greek yogurt
Grated zest and juice 2 lemons
3 tbsp fruit sugar
300g blueberries

Preheat the oven to 140°C, Gas Mark 2. Line a baking sheet with a sheet of non-stick silicone or baking parchment.

Using a very clean large bowl and an electric beater, whisk the egg whites with a pinch of salt until they form firm, floppy peaks. Gradually add the sugar in spoonfuls, whisking well between each spoonful until the mixture becomes a firm and glossy meringue. Then whisk in the cornflour and teaspoon of lemon juice.

Spoon the meringue on to the baking sheet in a large circle, approximately 25cm in diameter. Bake for up to 1 hour, until the outside is golden and the inside is soft like marshmallow. You can tell the meringue is ready because the paper will begin to peel away easily from the edge. Remove the pavlova shell, still on the paper to help keep it together, to a wire rack to cool. Then carefully peel off the paper and place on a large serving plate.

Beat the fruit sugar, zest and juice into the fromage frais. When you're ready to serve, spoon the mix into the centre of the pavlova. Scatter the blueberries over the top and serve, cut in wedges.

 Turn to pages 24, 68–9 and 139 for more recipes using blueberries

Vanilla cheesecakes with cassis and blackcurrant compote

Cheesecake is one of my favourite puddings. I love the creamy, sweet and slightly salty flavour, and with this blackcurrant and cassis sauce to cut through with its deep-purple colour and vitamin-C-laden flavour, it's even better.

The mini servings are very cute for tea parties or sweet canapés, but if you make them bigger they are of course brilliant puds in their own right!

Very cute for tea parties

Makes 20–24 petit-four size cheesecakes
Preparation time   25 minutes
Cooking time   15 minutes

125g reduced fat digestive biscuits
65g butter
200g light cream-cheese
50g fruit sugar
1 vanilla pod
3 tbsp soured cream
1 free-range egg
Grated zest ½ lemon
Juice ½ lemon
1 tsp pure vanilla extract

For the compote
300g frozen blackcurrants, or 340g canned blackcurrants, drained
50g fruit sugar
1 tbsp cassis

Crush the biscuits in a thick food-bag, twisting the top of the bag to seal them in. Bash the bag with a rolling pin until you have fine crumbs. Or you can blitz the biscuits in a food processor until fine.

Heat the oven to 180°C, Gas Mark 4. Melt the butter in a saucepan and mix in the biscuit crumbs. Divide the crumbs between 20–24 mini muffin tins (two 12-hole trays). Using the back of a teaspoon, press down on the crumbs and push them slightly up the sides to make little biscuit cups. Pat with the teaspoon until firm.

Beat the cream cheese and the sugar together until creamy. Slit the vanilla pod and scrape out the sticky seeds. Add these to the mixture along with the soured cream, egg, extract, lemon zest and juice. Spoon into the little cups – it doesn't matter if you spill a little.

Bake for 12–15 minutes or until just set. Leave to cool in the muffin tray for a couple of hours. In the meantime, make the compote. Place the blackcurrants in a saucepan with the sugar. Bring to the boil and then simmer for 2 minutes. Remove from the heat and stir in the cassis. Leave to cool then chill in the fridge till you're ready to serve. Demould the cheesecakes by running around the outside of each one with a small sharp knife. Serve with a small teaspoon of compote in the middle of each little cheesecake.

You can make the cheesecakes in bigger muffin trays for individual dessert-sized puddings.

Turn up the heat

APHRODISIAC DINNERS – IRRESISTIBLE LIGHT MEALS TO SEDUCE THAT CERTAIN SOMEONE

They do say that the way to a man's heart is through his stomach but we've all failed on at least one occasion to win over that certain someone so I'm not sure how much truth there is in the saying. (I think the phrase was coined before the invention of takeaways.) But it's worth trying everything you can to win his heart, though without looking like you are *actually* trying, of course.

There is an art of seduction when cooking tête-à-tête: it's all about the ritual of opening good wine, setting the scene and coming out of the kitchen holding exotic morsels, with your face slightly flushed from the heat.

So with this in mind, I've included some of my favourite 'bag the man' dishes here. One more piece of advice: never cook before the forth or fifth date. You should always have a few romantic dinners out first, when you can enjoy feeling spoilt. Also you don't want him to get used to it – don't give him too much of the good stuff too soon, he needs to appreciate you!

Lobster linguine

The dish of love! I challenge any man not to fall head over heels for you after eating this. You can vary the recipe according to how much you like him: if he really is the one, buy the lobsters alive and use the shells to infuse the sauce. Saying that, he has to be pretty special to get near this dish at all . . .

I challenge any man not to fall head over heels for you after eating this

Serves 2
Preparation time   10 minutes
Cooking time   30 minutes

1 large or 2 small lobsters, cooked, or you can use 300g large prawns
400ml tomato passata
1 tbsp olive oil
Small knob butter
1 onion, finely diced
2 cloves garlic, finely chopped
Pinch dried chillies
100g cherry tomatoes, halved
50ml brandy
2 tbsp double cream
250g dried linguine
Small bunch basil leaves

Cut the lobster down the centre lengthways and remove the pale cream meat. Reserve any liquid. Crack the claws with a lobster cracker or hit with the back of a heavy knife to open. Chop all the flesh into bite-size pieces, mix with any liquid saved and store in the fridge.

Heat the olive oil and butter in a deep frying pan and add the onion and garlic. Cook for about 5 minutes until translucent, then add the chilli, passata and cherry tomatoes. Fry for a further 5 minutes. Stir in the brandy and cook for another minute until the brandy evaporates. Season to taste. Mix in the cream and cook another minute or so.

To cook the pasta, put a large pan of water on to boil with a little salt. When it boils, pop the linguine into the water and cook according to pack instructions until it is *al dente*.

Chop the basil leaves and stir into the tomato sauce along with the lobster. Heat until almost boiling and then remove from the hob. Drain the pasta and then toss in the sauce. Reheat, check the seasoning and divide between two bowls.

Prawns and asparagus with lemon aioli

Prawns and asparagus are the typically tactile foods that are ideal to serve to a special loved one. They are perfect for feeding to each other and easy to make, so you'll have plenty of time to get ready, stress-free. This dish is very light and won't leave you feeling heavy.

Perfect for feeding to each other and easy to make

Serves 2
Preparation time   15 minutes
Cooking time   10 minutes

2 egg yolks, roughly beaten
1 tsp white wine vinegar
2 garlic cloves, roughly chopped
100ml olive oil
100ml other vegetable oil, such as corn oil
Juice ½ lemon (optional)
250g bunch asparagus spears
300g large king prawns, cooked (buy the best quality you can find)
Sea salt and freshly ground black pepper

Firstly, to make the aioli, put the yolks in a blender, along with the vinegar and roughly chopped garlic cloves. Blitz until fine and frothy.

Pour the two oils into a jug. With the blender blades still moving and the inner lid removed, pour in the oil in a very thin steady stream. The mixture will thicken and become mayonnaise-like. If it becomes too thick then add a squeeze of lemon juice or a splash of warm water. Season to taste, then scoop the mixture into a bowl or screw-top jar and chill until required.

Bring a large pan of water to the boil and add a little salt. Break off the woody ends of the asparagus and, using a swivel vegetable peeler, peel the ends if you want to (it's not vital). When the water is boiling rapidly, put in the asparagus and bring back to the boil. Simmer for 3–5 minutes depending on the thickness (you really don't want them overcooked though – we don't like droopy ones!). In the meantime get a large bowl of ice-cold water ready.

Drain the asparagus in a colander and slide them into the cold water. This stops the cooking. You can cool them further to serve cold or lightly warm. Arrange the prawns and asparagus on a platter with the aioli spooned into the centre.

 Turn to pages 94, 162–3 and 200 for more recipes using asparagus

Oysters Romanoff

Oysters are *the* aphrodisiac due to their high zinc level (good for men's fertility) and the tactile way they are eaten which just oozes sex appeal. I am a sucker for a plate of these with a glass of bubbly. Even though I am normally a purist when it comes to oysters and love them by themselves, the soured cream and caviar additions here are a luxury to melt any heart. It's very important to open oysters carefully though and to serve them ice cold.

Oysters are the ultimate aphrodisiac due to their high zinc level

Serves 2–4
Preparation time   10 minutes, plus time for opening oysters

12 oysters
3 spring onions, chopped very finely
2 lemons, for squeezing
3 tbsp soured cream
75g black caviar (the standard you buy is up to you, I suppose it depends on how keen you are! Lumpfish caviar is a more affordable option but still very tasty and can be found in most chiller cabinets)
Freshly ground black pepper

First, open the oysters (see page 87), keeping the liquid inside if possible. Lay the oysters flat on two or four plates. If you can, cover each plate with some rock salt – you can nestle the shells in the salt and this will hold them steady.

Sprinkle each oyster with spring onion then squeeze over a little lemon juice. Top with a tiny spoonful of soured cream and then a little caviar. Season with a few turns of black pepper and serve with love

Little love-bites of fig, almond and honey

This recipe came about because I didn't have the golden syrup and glacé cherries that are used in classic refrigerator cake. The end result was fantastic, though – the honey adds smoothness to the dish (and of course it is a natural sweetener) and the almonds and figs add an aphrodisiac love-note. I find that when you've had a big meal, these little chocolate love-bites are the perfect thing to feed to each other!

These little chocolate love-bites are the perfect thing to feed to each other!

Makes 35 or 70 biscuits
Preparation time   25 minutes

250g reduced-fat digestive biscuits
100g whole almonds
150g dried figs
50g ground almonds
5 tbsp runny honey
125g butter
100g chocolate, dark or light

Place the biscuits in a large, thick food-bag. Twist and seal the end and bash with a rolling pin until roughly crushed. You should aim to have a mixture of fine crumbs and little lumps. Depending on the size of your bag, you may have to do this in two batches.

Roughly chop the almonds into pieces approximately 5mm wide (you can do this in a food processor using the pulse button). Snip off the stalks from the figs and then cut the flesh into little pieces the same size as the nuts. Mix the whole almonds, ground almonds and figs with the biscuit crumbs.

Melt the butter with 3 tablespoons of honey (either in a small pan on the hob or in the microwave) then stir well into the crumb mix. Line the base of a shallow rectangular tin approximately 20x30cm with a strip of baking parchment. Tip in the crumb mix and spread around evenly, patting down with the back of a large spoon. Chill for at least an hour until firm.

Break up the chocolate and melt with the remaining honey either in a heatproof bowl over a pan of gently simmering water or in the microwave for 1–2 minutes, stirring until melted and smooth. Do not allow to overheat.

Using a teaspoon, drizzle the chocolate over (it doesn't need to cover the whole surface just roughly drizzled will be fine). Allow to set. Remove the whole mix from the tin and cut into 70 little 3cm squares or 35 larger 3x6cm fingers.

Turn to pages 144 and 166 for more recipes using figs

Quail on roasted butternut squash and asparagus with pomegranate and blood orange dressing

Seduction dinners are all about tactile, lick-the-fingers tasty morsels. Asparagus is a traditional aphrodisiac and great to pick up with your hands, and the same goes for quails, which must be picked up and eaten with the fingers, in a primeval manner.

Many years ago, spices were thought to raise the temperature and so be unsuitable for well-behaved ladies (like you and me), but I think the pink peppercorns add gentle sparkle and the pinks and reds of the dish blend wonderfully together. Finally, pomegranate, that decadent and time-consuming fruit: I'm in love with its jewel-like qualities and antioxidant merits. This dish will spin its magic and have you both happily entwined in no time!

Seduction dinners are all about tactile, lick-the-fingers tasty morsels

Serves 2 (any more for a romantic dinner is greedy and slightly too naughty!)
Preparation time   15 minutes
Cooking time   50 minutes

1 butternut squash
2 tbsp olive oil
2 quails, spatchcocked (ask your butcher for help)
½ tsp crushed pink peppercorns
Crushed sea salt
About 125g asparagus spears
½ small head radicchio

For the dressing
150ml blood-orange juice
2 tbsp good quality red wine vinegar
3 tbsp olive oil
½–1 tsp honey
2 tbsp picked pomegranate seeds

Firstly, preheat the oven to 180°C, Gas Mark 4. Then peel and cube the squash and lay out on a baking tray. Sprinkle the squash with olive oil and seasoning. Pop in the oven and cook for 40 minutes. While the squash is cooking, take the quails and rub with the crushed peppercorns and a good bit of sea salt. Place on another baking tray and pop in the oven for 30 minutes.

To make the dressing, pour the orange juice into a small saucepan, bring to the boil, turn down and simmer until reduced by half. Then whisk in the honey, vinegar and oil. Finally, add salt to taste and the pomegranate seeds.

Trim the woody stalks from the asparagus, rub with a little more oil and for the last 10 minutes of cooking time place on top of the squash.

Now all your components are ready, take two big white plates. Break the radicchio into leaves, arrange a few on to each plate, then add some squash and asparagus spears, lay the quail on the side and drizzle with the dressing.

CHEEKY MORSELS TO KEEP YOUR ENERGY UP

OK, so the aphrodisiac dinner worked and **you've gone well past dessert . . . lucky old you!** Maybe you're a few months down the line and in major Olympic gymnastic, honeymoon bliss – it's all good! If you need some brilliant energising bites that you can nonchalantly whip out, while still **looking like a sex kitten**, then these are for you.

Penne arrabiatta

If you want a red-hot quick dish to perk you up any time of the night or day, this is the one. Chillies have always been used to get people in the mood – they contain capaseine which naturally makes you feel happy so they are an ideal aphrodisiac. Pop on a pan of water, make this dish, serve it in little bowls and dive back in to bed . . .

A red-hot quick dish to perk you up anytime of the night or day

Serves 2
Preparation time   5 minutes
Cooking time   25 minutes

2 garlic cloves, roughly chopped
1 onion, diced
2 tbsp olive oil
1–2 big pinches dried chillies
Small glass white wine (left over from the night before, maybe!)
1 x 400g can chopped plum tomatoes
Pinch sugar
200g penne, or other pasta shapes
Freshly grated Parmesan cheese, to serve (optional)
Sea salt and freshly ground black pepper

Put around 2–3 litres of water on to boil in a large pan and add salt. Meanwhile, sweat the garlic and onion in the oil in a deep frying pan for about 3 minutes until translucent, then add the chilli (to taste) and cook for a further 2 minutes.

Stir in the wine and cook until reduced right down then mix in the tomatoes, sugar and seasoning. Simmer for a further 15 minutes.

By this time the pasta water should have reached boiling point. Stir in the penne and cook according to pack instructions until *al dente* (normally around 10–12 minutes). Be careful not to overcook. Drain and toss the pasta into the sauce. Reheat for another 2–3 minutes then serve sprinkled with Parmesan, if liked.

Mozzarella with fig and Parma ham

This is a classic dish that you can just chuck together from ingredients in the fridge. It's all about the soft texture of the torn mozzarella, the salty Parma ham and the bursting figs. Ultimately suggestive and sensual! Doubly great as you don't need to waste too much time cooking, so you can get back to more important things . . .

A classic dish that you can just chuck together

Serves 2
Preparation time 10 minutes

150g best mozzarella (such as mozzarella di bufala)
2 ripe figs
1 peach, halved and stoned
6 slices Parma ham, about 85-100g, or use Serrano or Bayonne ham
Small bunch basil
Little extra virgin olive oil (optional)
 Drizzle balsamic vinegar (optional)
Sea salt and freshly ground pepper

Slice up the mozzarella. Cut the peach and figs into wedges. Arrange all these on a platter and scrunch the ham attractively around. Roughly chop the basil and sprinkle over the platter. Drizzle with olive oil and balsamic vinegar, if liked, season with salt and pepper and serve. Simply delicious!

 Turn to pages 144 and 160–1 for more recipes using figs

MEALS TO IMPRESS
YOUR FAMILY … OR HIS

I'm not advocating being the little woman in the kitchen, but sometimes you just want to knock the socks off either your mother or, even more daunting, your mother-in-law or mother-in-law-to-be, **just to keep her quiet**. Be prepared for criticism though: even after twelve years as a chef and all my training I have still been told how to cook vegetables! Come to think of it, my own mother likes to remind me of basic cooking skills now and again . . . which always goes down well.

Never ever rise to the bait – it will make you look bad and put your family, your man or his mother (depending who it is you're cooking for) on the defensive. **Just smile and take a big gulp of wine while no one is looking**. You can sometimes go too far; remember, you mustn't look like you are trying to outshine anyone. One darling ex-boyfriend on hearing his mother comment on how my vegetables were undercooked replied that he actually like mine much better than hers! This will guarantee eternal hatred from aforementioned mother, especially if she's right (as I admit, in retrospect, she was).

Roasted monkfish and chorizo on sweet potato

I invented this dish for a pilot when I was just 17 and it hasn't lost its vibrancy. This dish is colourful and punchy and I love making it for a party. It's a Sunday lunch special too: instead of a leg of lamb I serve a whole monkfish.

This dish is colourful and punchy

Serves 4
Preparation time   20 minutes
Cooking time   1 hour

1 whole monkfish tail, about 800g, skinned and cleaned
2–3 sweet potatoes, about 600g in total
2 medium red onions
4 tbsp olive oil
20 slices chorizo
Sea salt and freshly ground black pepper

For the sauce
1 onion
3 cloves garlic
Pinch dried chilli flakes
400g can chopped tomatoes
Small handful coriander leaves
Small handful basil leaves
Sea salt and freshly ground black pepper

Before you start, make sure the fish is cleaned of any grey membrane. You can slice this off with a sharp knife. Cut the fillets away from the bone, if necessary.

Heat the oven to 200°C, Gas Mark 6. Peel and then cut the sweet potatoes into big chunks. Peel and cut the onions into eight pieces. Place the potato and onion in a large, shallow ovenproof dish, drizzle with half the olive oil and season with the salt and pepper. Pop the dish into the oven for 25 minutes, stirring once, until the potatoes are softened.

Meanwhile, make the sauce. Peel and dice the onion for the sauce and finely chop the garlic. Add the onion and garlic to a little saucepan with the remaining olive oil and fry until translucent. Add the chilli and the tomatoes. Season and bring to the boil, then simmer for 15 minutes. Set the sauce to one side.

Remove the potatoes from the oven, stir again. Lay the monkfish fillets on top of the potatoes, alternating the wide and thinner ends so you have one even block of fish. Lay the chorizo sausage slices on top overlapping like scales.

Return the dish to the oven and bake for a further 35 minutes or until the fish feels firm when pressed with the back of a fork. Remove and cool for 5 minutes then cut the fish into 4 portions and serve with the sweet potatoes, the sauce and a crisp green salad or lettuce and rocket.

Turn to page 131 for another recipe using chorizo

Lamb fillet with white bean crush and cumin carrots

White beans mash is fantastically healthy as the beans release energy slowly and contain great proteins and carbohydrates. The mash also goes really well with lots of other dishes; I serve it with white fish or chicken. The glossy, sweet beetroots and carrots are given another dimension by the spices – they're also great served cold, as a salad.

The glossy, sweet beetroots and carrots are given another dimension by the spices

Serves 4
Preparation time   30 minutes
Cooking time   45 minutes

4 lamb neck fillets, about 125g each
250g baby beetroots, roots trimmed
1 whole bulb garlic
1x400g can butter beans
3 tbsp olive oil
1 tsp cinnamon
1 tsp cumin
1 tsp coriander
250g baby carrots, trimmed
1 tbsp honey
Small handful flat-leaf parsley leaves
2 sprigs fresh rosemary
50g pine nuts, toasted
Sea salt and freshly ground black pepper

Preheat the oven to 200°C, Gas Mark 6. Trim the lamb of any fat or sinews and set aside. Pop the beetroot in a baking dish, cover with foil and roast for about 45 minutes or until cooked through. At the same time, roast the garlic (see my rack of lamb recipe on page 106) then pop the soft flesh into a saucepan. Drain the beans and add to the pan with 2 tbsp water and 1 tbsp of oil. Heat until bubbling then blitz with a handheld blender to a smooth purée or mash with a fork for a chunkier consistency.

Heat a large sauté pan and add the remaining olive oil, spices and herbs. Then add the carrots and cover in the oil and spice mix. Season and add 200ml of water. Bring to the boil and simmer until the carrots are tender and the water has evaporated. Add the honey, beetroot and parsley and keep warm.

Strip the rosemary of its leaves and scatter over a clean chopping board. Season the lamb and roll in the rosemary. Heat a non-stick pan with 1 tbsp of oil and cook the lamb until golden brown on the outside and pink in the middle. This should take around 10 minutes. Remove the pan from the heat and leave to stand for 5 minutes.

Reheat the bean mash and vegetables. Slice the lamb into medallions. Serve the lamb on top of the mash with the vegetables on the side and a sprinkling of pine nuts.

Veal rolls with lemon and olives

Veal is a pale and lightly flavoured meat; the strong anchovies, olives and lemons really complement it. Don't be put off by the anchovies if you're worried they might be too fishy – their savoury flavour works really well here.

Don't be put off by the anchovies . . . their savoury flavour works really well

Serves 4
Preparation time   15 minutes
Cooking time   45 minutes

1 butternut squash, about 750g
2 tbsp olive oil
8 small veal escalopes, about 100g each, thinly cut
8 anchovies, patted dry
100g green olives, stoned and chopped
2 cloves garlic, chopped
Juice 2 lemons
100ml vegetable stock (can be made with a cube)
1 tsp cornflour
25g butter
Small handful flat-leaf parsley
Cavelo Nero (black Italian cabbage), to serve (or try Savoy cabbage)
Sea salt and freshly ground black pepper

Preheat the oven to 180°C, Gas Mark 4. Halve and deseed the squash. Cut it into chunks and peel – it's easier to do it this way round rather than peel a whole squash. Place the squash on a roasting tray, drizzle with the oil and season. Roast for about 30 minutes until softened.

Meanwhile, lay a veal escalope on a clean chopping board, place an anchovy down the centre, roll up and secure with a toothpick. Repeat with the other escalopes. Heat a large sauté pan with 2 tbsp of oil and brown the veal all over, for about 5 minutes. Add the olives and garlic to the pan and continue cooking for 2–3 minutes. Stir in the lemon juice and the stock. Bring to the boil then turn down the heat and simmer for 10 minutes until tender. The veal may not need any salt, due to the anchovies and olives, but a little pepper works well.

Remove the veal rolls to a plate. Blend the cornflour with 1 tbsp of water and then whisk into the pan juices. Add the butter to the sauce in knobs, stirring until smooth. Remove the toothpicks from the rolls and return them to the pan. Reheat gently and scatter over the parsley. Serve with the roasted squash and some nicely boiled or steamed Cavelo Nero.

Cranachan parfait

Crana-what? I hear you say . . . this is a traditional Scottish pudding. The combination of whipped cream, caramelised oats, whisky and raspberries is heaven. I have changed it by making it into a parfait – it's a very simple way to make an alternative to ice cream and you'll soon want to have it on standby in the future!

The combination of whipped cream, caramelised oats, whisky and raspberries is heaven

Serves 4
Preparation time 30 minutes
Cooking time 20 minutes, plus 2-4 hours freezing time

100g butter
150g light muscovado sugar
200g jumbo porridge oats
300g fresh raspberries, plus extra to serve
2 tsp icing sugar or 1 tsp fruit sugar
5 tablespoons whisky
450ml double cream, or half cream, half low-fat set yogurt
3 egg yolks
3 tbsp fruit sugar

Preheat the oven to 180°C, Gas Mark 4. Melt the butter in a frying pan and then stir in the muscovado sugar. Cook until the sugar has melted and then mix in the oats. Spread the mixture out on a baking sheet and bake for 15–20 minutes. Twice during cooking, take the sheet out of the oven and use a wooden spoon to separate the oats so they become crisp. Remove from the oven after cooking and allow to cool.

In a bowl, mix the raspberries and icing sugar together, then sprinkle in 2 tablespoons of the whisky and set aside. In a larger bowl and using an electric whisk (or balloon whisk), whisk the double cream until it forms soft peaks. Gradually add the remaining whisky and set aside. (If using a half-yogurt mix, whisk the cream separately then fold in the set yogurt).

In another bowl, whisk the egg yolks and fruit sugar together until pale and fluffy. Fold into the cream mix.

Line a 500g loaf tin with clingfilm. Fold the raspberries and oats into the cream mix and pour into the tin. Freeze for 2–4 hours.

Take the parfait out of the freezer 5 minutes before serving, remove the clingfilm and cut into slices with a hot knife. Pop the slices on to a plate and serve with a little pile of the extra raspberries.

Tropical trifle

I adore trifle but it can be very rich. This is a super lower calorie version, using my favourite coconut milk as custard and lots of fresh tropical fruit. The flavours are great – a little slice of paradise – and the snowy coconut and tangy passion fruits look beautiful.

A little slice of paradise

Serves 6-8
Preparation time 25 minutes
Cooking time 20 minutes

For the sponge
3 large free-range eggs, separated
125g caster sugar
1 tsp vanilla extract
90g self-raising flour
½ tsp sea salt

For the topping
400g can reduced-fat coconut milk
25g desiccated coconut
50g light muscovado sugar
1 tbsp cornflour
2 ripe medium-size mangoes
Juice 1 lime
1 tbsp Malibu
150ml double cream
4 ripe passion fruits

Line the base of a Swiss-roll tin (about 30x23cm) with a sheet of non-stick baking paper, allowing a little paper to hang over the sides of the tin. Preheat the oven to 180°C, Gas Mark 4.

In a large mixing bowl, beat together the egg yolks, half the sugar and the vanilla using an electric whisk until the mixture is pale, thick and fluffy. Sift together the flour and salt in another bowl and then fold into the egg mix.

Whip the egg whites in a separate bowl until they form soft but firm peaks. Then beat in the remaining sugar to make a meringue. Using a large metal spoon, fold this meringue mixture into the egg and flour mix and then scoop into the prepared tin, spreading to the edges. Bake for 10–12 minutes until golden and firm when pressed.

Remove from the oven and leave to cool upside down on a wire rack. When cold, peel off the paper. Cut the sponge into 3cm wide fingers and arrange at the bottom of a trifle bowl.

To make the coconut custard, heat the coconut milk, sugar and desiccated coconut in a large non-stick saucepan. Blend the cornflour with 2 tbsp of cold water in a small jug. When the milk is on the point of boiling, pour a little into the cornflour and stir to blend. Then pour the cornflour mix back into the pan of very hot milk and, with the pan back on the heat, whisk well for a few seconds until the custard thickens. Remove from the heat and leave to cool, stirring occasionally to prevent a skin forming.

While the custard is cooling, prepare the fruit. Peel and slice the mangoes and scatter the slices over the sponge fingers. Sprinkle over the lime juice and Malibu. When the custard is cold, spoon this over the top of the mangoes.

Whip the cream until almost stiff and dollop over the coconut custard – it doesn't have to be in an even layer. Halve the passion fruits and dribble the seedy pulp on top of the trifle. Chill until ready to serve.

Plum, cinnamon and soured cream tart

You can't beat a good tart! This tempting one is fantastic and very easy to make. It really is a family dish too and will smell amazing when baking. It is a perfect autumnal treat. You could also replace the plums with apples.

You can't beat a good tart!

Makes 6 slices

Preparation time 12 minutes, plus time for baking blind

Cooking time 50 minutes

1 ready-made pastry case, about 20cm diameter
400g ripe red or pink plums (about 6 plums)
300ml soured cream
50g pecans, roughly chopped
100g dark muscovado sugar
1 tsp cinnamon
Baking beans, for baking blind, if necessary

If your pastry case is uncooked then pre-heat the oven to 190°C, Gas Mark 5. Line the pastry case with a large sheet of baking parchment and fill with baking beans. Place the case on a metal baking sheet and bake for 15 minutes. Remove the beans and paper and return the case to the oven for a further 5 minutes. Remove and leave to cool. (This is known as baking blind, should you need to know for another time!)

Slice the plums in half around the stones, twist the halves to separate and then remove the stones. Slice the plums into 6–8 wedges and mix with the soured cream. Tip this mixture into the pastry case and spread evenly.

Sprinkle the pecans, then the sugar and cinnamon over the mixture. Bake the tart for about 30 minutes until the top is nicely browned and bubbling. Remove from the oven and leave to cool for 30–40 minutes to let the tart firm up. Cut into six and serve.

Quick fixes to fit into that little black dress or bikini

ONE-WEEK COUNTDOWN TILL THAT SPECIAL OCCASION

I am the last person on the planet to advocate a crash diet, and this is by no means one. There are times, though, when you want to look super bright-eyed and bushy-tailed, maybe for a special occasion. So this is **a good week-long dinner plan if you're looking for a bit of a boost**. I try to stick to it before filming or a photo shoot and it's always useful if there is a possibility you might bump into **that nasty ex** at a party or wedding.

This is not a plan for life, though — it's delicious for a week but beyond that it may get boring, and there is **nothing more boring than a glamorous girl on a diet**.

Baked sweet potatoes with avocado butter

Baked potatoes are one of those foods that have an old-fashioned comfort and ease-factor, yet in all honesty can pile on the pounds and are well behind in the nutrition stakes.

I love sweet potatoes: their vibrant orange hues and sweet fudgey texture comfort me. Instead of using high-fat butter I make a delightful pale green accompaniment from avocadoes that has the richness in your mouth, but contains good fats that help give you a healthy heart instead. I always get terribly depressed when I hear someone saying how high in fat and calorific avocadoes are, and how they are best avoided. Boo hoo! Avocadoes are rich in healthy low-cholesterol fats and are good for you, just as nature intended – and that's it!

Avocadoes are rich in healthy low-cholesterol fats and are good for you

Serves 2
Preparation time   10 minutes
Cooking time   1 hour

2 large orange sweet potatoes,
about 300g each
1 large ripe avocado
Small handful coriander, roughly chopped
2 spring onions, chopped
Juice 1 lime
Sweet chilli sauce, to serve
Sea salt and freshly ground black pepper

Preheat the oven to 190°C, Gas Mark 5. Scrub the potatoes and score a line on the skin of each one. Put the potatoes on the middle shelf of the oven and bake for about 1 hour or until you can prick them with a thin-bladed knife and feel they have softened.

Meanwhile, mash the avocado with a fork. Add the coriander, onions, lime juice and seasoning. When the potatoes are cooked, slit the tops and open up. Spoon in the avocado and drizzle with the sweet chilli sauce. Yum yum!

Turn to pages 19, 58 and 168-9 for more recipes using sweet potato

Miso salmon with black-sesame pickled vegetables and steamed rice

Nobu is one of my favourite restaurants and although the dishes are very complex there, I try and make this cheats' version of their black cod at home. I believe that the black cod and edamame pods there are the only sustenance that the fashion pack consume, especially during London Fashion Week, so if it's skinny enough for them . . . You feel very virtuous while eating this and there is just the right balance of sweet miso, clean rice and gentle pickles.

You feel very virtuous eating this

Serves 2
Marinating time up to 24 hours
Preparation time   15 minutes
Cooking time   15 minutes

2 fillets salmon, about 120g each. I love Alaskan wild salmon or organic

For the marinade
2 tbsp sweet rice miso
1½ tsbp soy sauce
1 tsp honey
1 tsp mirin

Japanese pickles
1 small carrot
½ mouli (Japanese white radish) – if available
Sea salt, to sprinkle
½ cucumber
100ml rice vinegar
1 tsp sugar
25g pickled pink ginger
½ – 1 tsp black sesame seeds

150g Jasmine or basmati rice

Mix all the marinade together in a bowl, then spread over the fish fillets in a dish and leave for at least an hour or overnight if possible.

Peel the carrot and mouli and then cut into fine julienne strips, place in a bowl and sprinkle with salt. Cut the cucumber in half lengthways and scoop out the seeds with a teaspoon, then slice thinly on the diagonal. Place in a bowl with the carrot and mouli and mix all together, rubbing in the salt slightly. Leave for twenty minutes.

Pour the vinegar into a saucepan and add the sugar, heat gently and simmer for 5 minutes.

Thoroughly rinse the salt off the vegetables in cold water then pat dry and cover with the cooled vinegar mix. Cut the ginger into strips, add to the vegetables and then chill.

Then cook the rice (as a general rule I use twice as much water as rice). Bring to the boil and simmer with the lid on, until the water is absorbed. Remove the pan from the heat and leave to stand, still covered, for 5 minutes.

To cook the salmon, heat the grill up very high and grill for 5 minutes on each side until charred on the outside and pinkish in the middle. Then serve the salmon with the pickles (I like to add a sprinkling of black sesame seed to the pickle) and rice. A little roughly chopped coriander would also be nice.

Thai chicken soup

Chicken soup has long been described as food for the soul, and I definitely believe it is: I'll stop at nothing when I need a dose. It's frustrating that you can't buy the same good-quality fresh chicken soup here as you can in New York, where it really does help you get over flu and colds. I have added chilli, garlic and ginger to this – great boosts for your metabolism. And perfect when you're trying to shape up!

Perfect when you're trying to shape up!

Serves 4–6
Preparation time 15 minutes
Cooking time Up to 2 hours

1 organic free-range chicken, around 1.5kg (or whatever fits in your pot)
1 red chilli, slit and deseeded
2 shallots
2 sticks lemongrass
5cm piece fresh root ginger
5cm piece fresh galangal, if you can get it
2 garlic cloves
2 shallots
3 kaffir lime leaves
Small bunch coriander, leaves and stalks separated
1 strip lime zest
1 tbsp Thai fish sauce
100g thin rice noodles
½ tsp sugar
Sea salt and freshly ground black pepper

Firstly, untie the chicken legs and discard any string. Then pull out the pad of fat from inside the body cavity. Place the chicken in your biggest pot. Roughly chop the aromatic flavourings from the chilli to the lime zest (reserve the coriander leaves) and add to the pot, along with the coriander stalks.

Cover everything in cold water, about 4 litres if you can get it in. Bring slowly to the boil, then turn right down to a gentle simmer. Cook uncovered for about 1 ½ to 2 hours until the bird is very tender and the stock reduced down by half.

Strain off the stock into another large saucepan. Discard the aromatic flavourings. Cool and skin the chicken. Pull the legs and thighs away and use these in another dish (such as a chicken pie filling or for a pasta sauce). Remove the two breasts and pull into fine shreds. Discard all the bones.

Add the rice noodles, chopped coriander leaves, fish sauce and sugar to the reserved stock and return to a boil. Simmer for 5 minutes, stir in the shredded chicken, simmer for another 5 minutes then check the seasoning and serve.

Sardines on peperonata

My general thought is brightly-coloured food equals nutrients and taste – and it's so true. The grey ready-made foods in supermarkets are somehow so sad and miss the point of eating entirely.

I'm not saying food should be thought of purely in terms of nutrients (although it's not a bad thought) but it should always be thought of in terms of beauty and taste. This dish is my ray of sunshine: the peppers, saffron and tomatoes scream sunny holidays, as do the lightly grilled, oily little sardines.

Keeping on the nutrition tack, sardines are high in oh-so-friendly Omega 3 oils, good for shiny locks and glowing skin. To make sure your sardines are fresh, check for bright eyes and firm flesh. If you need to skin them, remove the scales by rubbing the fish with your thumb under cold running water.

Brightly-coloured food equals nutrients and taste

Serves 2
Preparation time   15 minutes
Cooking time   30 minutes

6 very fresh small sardines, heads removed, and gutted
1 red pepper, finely sliced
1 yellow pepper, finely sliced
2 cloves garlic, chopped
1 onion, finely sliced
2 tbsp olive oil
2 plum tomatoes, quartered
1 pinch saffron
1 tsp sugar, ideally fruit sugar
1 tbsp small capers
1 tbsp roughly chopped basil
Sea salt and freshly ground black pepper

Before you start, double-check the sardines are really fresh. If you're happy with them, wash their insides under cold running water and pat dry.

Sweat the peppers, onion and garlic in the olive oil for about 8–10 minutes until they start to soften. Add the plum tomatoes, saffron, sugar, and salt to taste then cook for about 20 minutes to a pulpy mixture. This makes a peperonata. Stir in the basil and capers. Check the seasoning and set aside.

Meanwhile, preheat the grill until very hot. Season the sardines and grill for 3–4 minutes on each side until just firm when pressed with the back of a fork.

Reheat the peperonata and serve with the sardines on the side. Delicious with crusty bread.

Quinoa with tandoori chicken

Quinoa is a strange little grain that originated in South America. It's very high in protein and amino acids, and is also great for those with a gluten intolerance. Some call it the Inca super-grain. I love its tiny globe-like appearance (have a close look at it when cooked) and its nutty flavour. It's not used a lot in the UK, but is definitely worth trying out. I have paired it with yogurt-glazed spiced chicken, a tangy sauce and a chilli-infused salsa. This dish is very low in fat but still feels like a satisfying meal.

Very low in fat but still feels like a satisfying meal

Serves 2

Preparation time   20 minutes, plus marinating for 1 hour

Cooking time   30 minutes

1 150g pot natural yogurt
2 tsp tandoori paste
Large bunch coriander, about 30g
1 garlic clove, crushed
1 tsp mango chutney
1 skinless, boneless organic chicken breast, about 150g, cut into medium strips
150g quinoa
400ml chicken stock (can be made with a cube or bouillon powder)
2 cardamom pods
Pinch saffron strands
Sea salt and freshly ground black pepper

For the mint-yogurt sauce

2 tbsp natural yogurt
Small bunch mint, leaves picked off
Juice ½ lemon

For the tomato and chilli salsa

2 tomatoes
½ small red onion, finely chopped
1 green chilli, slit, deseeded and chopped

Mix together half the pot of yogurt and tandoori paste in a large shallow bowl. Finely chop the leaves from half the coriander and mix in along with the garlic and mango chutney. Then mix in the chicken pieces and leave for about 1 hour.

While that is marinating, make the serving sauces. Finely chop the mint leaves and mix with the remaining yogurt, lemon juice and seasoning. Chill until ready to serve.

For the salsa, halve the tomatoes, remove the cores then finely chop the flesh. Mix with the onion and chilli, season and set aside.

Cook the quinoa, according to packet instructions, with the stock in a covered pan adding the cardamom and saffron. Remove from the heat when cooked and leave in a covered pan, while you cook the chicken. Discard the cardamom.

Heat a non-stick griddle pan until very hot. Scrape off excess paste from the chicken, season then cook for about 6 minutes. Turn with tongs to try and get black charcoal lines from the griddle pan on the chicken for flavour and make sure it is cooked through. Serve the chicken strips on the quinoa with the sauce and salsa.

Balinese spiced fish with coconut rice

Bali has always been a huge inspiration to me. I lived there for a while when I was younger and have been back many times. Bali has a gentleness to it, the people are lovely and I love the food there. Discovering the new flavours of young green coconuts, spices and hot chillies was a real foodie eye-opener for me, at the age of eleven.

These ingredients are slightly simplified versions from a Bali dish to make the recipe easy to make. If you have a good Thai or Oriental supermarket in your area, pop by and you'll be able to pick fresh ingredients at great prices.

These ingredients are slightly simplified versions from a Bali dish

Serves 2

Preparation time   10 minutes,
                       plus marinating time

Cooking time   25 minutes

2 cod steaks, about 125g each
150g Thai jasmine rice, raw
50ml reduced-fat coconut milk
1 lime, halved to serve

For the spice paste
3cm piece galangal (if you can't find this use fresh root ginger)
2 garlic cloves
1 small red chilli, slit and deseeded
½ tsp turmeric
½ tsp shrimp paste (or 1tsp Thai fish sauce)
1 shallot, finely sliced
2 kaffir lime leaves, dried or fresh, roughly snipped with scissors

Firstly, to make the paste blitz the galangal, garlic, chilli, turmeric, shrimp paste and shallot in a blender until smooth. Then scrape into a bowl and add the kaffir lime leaves. Rub this spice paste on to both sides of the fish steaks. Set aside while you cook the rice. For a deeper flavour, marinate overnight.

Put the rice into a pan with 300ml water (though without salt) and the coconut milk. Bring to the boil, then cover and simmer on a low heat for 10 minutes. Remove the pan from the heat and set aside for 5 minutes, still covered, while you cook the fish.

Preheat the grill. Remove the fish from the marinade, scraping off any excess, season and place on a heavy baking sheet and grill for 5 minutes on each side, or until just firm when pressed with the back of a fork. Serve the fish with the lime wedges and a pile of rice.

Chargrilled fennel chicken on courgette and carrot

Chicken is a great food to detox with as it is very easily digested. The fennel seeds in this dish also aid digestion, so it's a brilliant one to pull out of the bag when you need that cleansing feeling.

The colourful ribbons of carrot and courgette make the plate look beautiful and if you add some boiled rice this dish will be a substantial dinner by anyone's standards!

A brilliant one to pull out of the bag when you need that cleansing feeling

Serves 2
Preparation time   10 minutes
Cooking time   15 minutes

2 medium courgettes, trimmed
2 medium carrots, peeled
2 organic skinless, boneless chicken breasts,
about 125g each
3 tbsp olive oil
1 tsp fennel seeds
Juice 1 orange
Sea salt and freshly ground black pepper

Prepare a large bowl of iced water and leave to one side. Make ribbons of carrot and courgette by drawing a swivel vegetable peeler down the length of the vegetables. Have a large pan of boiling water on the stove and blanch the ribbons for 2 minutes until wilted. Drain the vegetables and immediately plunge them into the iced water. Drain again and set aside.

Cut the chicken part-way through down the middle and open up to resemble a butterfly. Rub with the fennel seeds and some seasoning and brush the outside with oil.

Heat a griddle pan and cook the chicken over a medium heat for 5–7 minutes on each side until just firm when pressed. While the chicken is cooking, gently heat about 2 tbsp of olive oil in a medium sauté pan. Add the courgettes, carrots and orange juice. Cook for about 5 minutes until the orange juice is reduced by half. Season and serve with the chicken breasts.

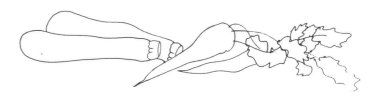

TOO-MUCH-PARTYING DETOX FOOD

Feel like death warmed up? Skin lost its glow? Can't face another party – what? **Can't face another party? It must be bad!**

Before you rush to the phone and dial 999, don't worry, it's OK, it happens to even the most fabulous glamorous girls. There are times when too much of a good thing really is too much. Though **we all love food,** we sometimes forget that it's there to fuel and nourish us, not drown us in empty calories. Here are **my little tips for feeling better** when a little sluggish and bloated.

Butternut squash, orange and ginger soup

This soup is a real comforter, yet super healthy. Orange and yellow vegetables contain beta-carotene, which converts into vitamin E and is great for your eyes. On top of this, the soup tastes good, the ginger adds warmth to it and it will fill you up.

This soup is a real comforter, yet super healthy

Serves 4
Preparation time   10 minutes
Cooking time   40 minutes

2 tbsp olive oil
1 onion, chopped
1 garlic clove, finely chopped
5cm piece fresh root ginger, finely chopped
1 butternut squash, about 1kg
1 litre vegetable stock (can be made with a cube)
Small handful fresh coriander leaves
Juice and zest 1 orange
Sea salt and freshly ground black pepper

Heat up a heavy-based saucepan and add the olive oil. Gently fry the onions, garlic and ginger for about 5 minutes until translucent.

Meanwhile, peel, deseed and dice the squash. Add to the pan along with the stock and bring to the boil. Turn down and simmer for 30–40 minutes until softened. Crush the squash slightly with a fork by pressing against the side of the pan for a thickened texture. Check the seasoning, add the orange juice and zest and the coriander leaves and blitz with a handheld blender. Serve hot!

Miso seafood soup

Miso is a wonderful flavourful paste made from soya beans. We used to eat a lot of miso soup when I was little and have crispy toasted nori seaweed in packed lunches! Although I was always jealous of my friends' jam sandwiches, now I see miso's appeal.

I've added seafood to this recipe to make it into a main meal.

Serves 2
Preparation time   5 minutes
Cooking time   5 minutes

3cm piece ginger, grated
1 red chilli, slit and deseeded
100g squid rings, thawed, if frozen
4–6 raw king prawns
6–8 raw large peeled prawns
2 tbsp miso paste, or use 2 miso soup packs
2 sheets nori seaweed, torn by hand, or dried
Wakame seaweed
1 tsp soy sauce
(or use Tamari for wheat-free soy)
2 spring onions, sliced
2 crabsticks, sliced

Put the ginger and chilli in a saucepan with 500ml of water. Bring to the boil then reduce the heat and add the squid and prawns. Simmer for 1 minute and then stir in the miso. Finally add the seaweed, tamari and sliced spring onions.

To serve, place the sliced crab sticks in two warmed soup bowls and pour over the hot soup with all the ingredients in.

Brown rice with lentils, caramelised onion and Greek yogurt

Lentils. Nothing glam about those, I hear you cry! Well this dish has slow energy-releasing carbohydrates from the rice and fat-free protein from the lentils. It's also one of those dishes that I crave when I've overdone it. The parsley is a cleansing herb and the yogurts contain good bacteria.

Serves 2
Preparation time   5 minutes
Cooking time   40 minutes

150g brown rice
50g puy lentils
750ml vegetable stock (can be made with a cube or bouillon powder)
Small handful flat-leaf parsley
1 tbsp caramelised onion marmalade or onion relish
2 tbsp 0% fat Greek yogurt
Sea salt and freshly ground black pepper

Put the rice and lentils into a saucepan and cover with the stock. Put on the lid, bring to the boil and simmer for 40–45 minutes or until the rice and lentils are cooked and all the stock has been absorbed.

Roughly chop the parsley and stir through, along with the onion marmalade. Then check the seasoning and serve with a dollop of Greek yogurt.

Turn to pages 64-5 and 134 for more recipes using yogurt

Chargrilled turkey steaks with chilli and garlic broccoli

Chargrilling is a really good low-fat way of cooking – you use minimal oil and the charred lines give you added flavour. You can chargrill any meat and most fish.

After this home-cooked meal, I feel great knowing I'm getting all good nutrients. Turkey and broccoli are both superfoods. Turkey is a great protein, very low in fat and high in zinc, potassium and vitamin B. Broccoli is full of vitamins B and C, too. The chilli and garlic are both metabolism boosters.

After this home-cooked meal, I feel great knowing I'm getting all good nutrients

Serves 2
Preparation time   10 minutes
Cooking time   12 minutes

150g tender-stem or purple sprouting broccoli
2 turkey steaks, about 125g each
1 tbsp olive oil
2 cloves garlic, finely sliced
1 pinch dried chillies or chilli powder
½ lemon, cut into wedges
Sea salt and freshly ground black pepper

Heat a griddle pan until very hot and put a saucepan of water on to boil. Blanch the broccoli in the water for two minutes, then drain. Cool under cold running water for 1 minute to cool and refresh.

Season the turkey steaks on each side and lay in the very hot griddle pan for 4 minutes on each side. Cover and leave to rest on a plate.

Heat a little olive oil in a wok and add the garlic and chilli. Cook for 2 minutes, until the garlic is just starting to brown, then add the broccoli. Stir-fry for 5 minutes and then serve with the turkey and lemon wedges.

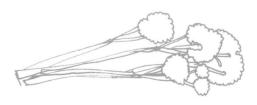

Poached chicken and Asian coleslaw

I feel fantastic when I eat food like this – simple and fresh flavours have a real clarity. This dish can be served as a very light supper or lunch that can be eaten as it is or with the addition of steamed rice. Believe me, stick to a week of this and you will be feeling bright-eyed and bushy-tailed in no time!

Simple and fresh flavours have a real clarity

Serves 2
Preparation time   10 minutes
Cooking time   25 minutes

450ml chicken stock (can be made with a cube or bouillon powder)
2 organic chicken breasts, about 125g each
5cm piece fresh root ginger
1 shallot, thinly sliced
½ Chinese cabbage
Small handful mint leaves
Small handful basil leaves
1 tsp sweet chilli sauce
1 tsp light soy sauce
Juice 1 lime

Heat the stock in a medium-size frying or sauté pan deep enough to contain the two chicken breasts. Add the chicken, roughly chopped ginger and shallot. Bring to the boil then turn down to a very low simmer and cook for 10–15 minutes, until just firm when pressed with a fork. It's very important to make sure the chicken is cooked through properly. Then strain the stock and reserve, discarding the ginger and shallot.

Return the stock to the pan and keep at a high boil until reduced down by at least half. Remove and leave to cool while you make the salad.

Cut out the core of the cabbage and then slice the leaves very finely. Combine the cabbage with the herb leaves. Then mix with the hot reduced stock, chilli sauce and soy sauce so the leaves just wilt, and divide between two plates. Slice the chicken and serve on the warm salad with the lime squeezed over.

Sesame-crusted tuna carpaccio with soy and mustard dressing

Carpaccio is a great dish to order in a restaurant when you're watching your figure. The tuna version is really simple to make at home and it looks very impressive; I love the deep red, rare tuna and two-tone sesame crust. It's great as a starter, part of a main course or even part of a special buffet or picnic.

Really simple to make at home and it looks very impressive

Serves 4
Preparation time   5 minutes
Cooking time   10 minutes

500g best tuna loin (it needs to be fresh, as it is served pretty well raw)
1 tbsp sesame seeds
1 tbsp black onion seeds
Sea salt flakes
1 tbsp olive oil
1 small head radicchio (or a big bag of mixed salad that has some red leaves)
1 small head chicory
2 spring onions, sliced
100g cherry tomatoes, halved

For the dressing
1 tsp wholegrain mustard
½ tsp wasabi
1 tbsp soy sauce
1 tsp honey
2 tsp rice vinegar
1 tsp light olive oil
Splash sesame oil

Trim the tuna loin so it is a nice even shape. Mix the dressing ingredients by shaking everything together in a screw-top jar. Set aside.

Mix the two types of seeds together in a bowl with a teaspoon of sea salt flakes and some ground black pepper. Then tip the mix on to a plate. Roll the tuna in the mix until evenly coated.

Heat the oil in a large frying pan and seal the tuna evenly on all sides. You want to have a golden crust on the outside and this should take no more than about 4 minutes in total. The tuna should be just browned on the outside and still rare in the centre. Remove the tuna from the pan and leave to cool.

Discard the outer leaves of the radicchio and chicory, and break the inner leaves into pieces. Finely slice the spring onions and halve the tomatoes.

To serve, slice the tuna as thinly as possible with a razor-sharp knife and lay on a platter. Arrange the salad next to the slices and drizzle the dressing over everything.

RECIPES FOR DIETRY RESTRICTIONS

Though I have suffered from ME since I was fourteen, I am one of the lucky ones in so far as I live **a packed life** with a pretty high level of energy. I do watch what I eat though, and must recuperate when I need to. Wheat is a big no-no for me and I know a lot of people who have reactions to certain other foods.

Many of the recipes in this book are great for all sorts of dietary restrictions but in this section are more unusual recipes. I hate it when you see labels on shop-bought food – like 'fat-free' on a packet of jelly. Of course it's fat free, it's bloomin' jelly! **Wheat-free cake, though, is another story.** Here are some recipes that won't leave you or your friends with dietary restrictions feeling left out or neglected.

Flourless hazelnut cake

My mother is a great cook but never gets on so well with cakes. There was one though that always came out on my birthday. This hazelnut cake is now one of my favourites and I love it. You can serve it by itself or with whipped cream . . . depending on how naughty you feel! And it's perfect for those on a wheat-free diet.

This hazelnut cake is now one of my favourites and I love it

Makes one cake to serve 6
Preparation time   10 minutes
Cooking time   40 minutes

285g hazelnuts (you can use almonds or pistachios, if preferred)
300g caster sugar
8 egg whites

Preheat the oven to 190°C, Gas Mark 5. Lightly oil the base of a deep, 20cm round cake tin and line with parchment paper. Blitz the nuts and sugar together in a food processor to blend and mix well.

Whisk the egg whites to soft peaks then gently fold in the nut mixture. Scoop the mix into the tin and bake for about 40 minutes until pale and golden on top. Leave to cool, turn out of the tin and dust with icing sugar.

Parmesan crispy chicken with tomato, avocado and sweetcorn salsa

Crispy fried chicken is one of those foods that you just crave sometimes. It was pretty much off-limits to my wheat-free diet until I started to make it with cornmeal. Essentially, the bits you crave are still there – the moist meat, slightly spicy coating and the freshly fried flavour. I've added a hint of Californian style with a bright and colourful salsa, but you can serve it with anything.

A hint of Californian style with a bright and colourful salsa

Serves 2
Preparation time 20 minutes
Cooking time 15 minutes

1 fresh small corn cob
1 avocado, halved, stoned, peeled and cut in fine dice
1 red onion, finely diced
Juice 1 lime
150g cherry tomatoes, halved
Small handful fresh coriander, roughly chopped
1 large free-range egg
2 tbsp milk
2 skinless and boneless organic chicken breasts, about 125g each, cut in strips
100g cornmeal or polenta
1 tsp smoked paprika
½ tsp garlic powder
50g freshly grated Parmesan
3 tbsp olive oil, for frying
Sea salt and freshly ground black pepper

Stand the corn cob upright and, using a sharp knife, cut down to release the kernels. Mix, raw, in a bowl with the onion, avocado, lime juice, tomatoes and roughly chopped coriander.

Beat the egg and milk together in a shallow dish and drop in the chicken pieces, mixing well. In a separate shallow dish, mix the polenta, garlic powder, paprika and Parmesan together. Then, drain the chicken and coat each piece evenly with the polenta mix.

Heat the olive oil in a frying pan up to a medium heat with and pan-fry the chicken strips for about 8 to 10 minutes, turning once, until golden brown and crispy. Then drain and serve with a pile of the salsa on the side.

A low-carb tart (No, not me . . .)

I first invented this dish when a celebrity client wanted a goats' cheese tartlet without the pastry. Always up for an impossible challenge, I developed this. Using the artichoke as the case means you get the flavour from the artichoke, which goes perfectly with the filling, without the drawbacks of soggy pastry and lots of carbohydrates. I often serve this as a starter or a lovely spring lunch and I experiment with different fillings too, such as crab and tarragon, or asparagus and goats' cheese.

Serve this as a starter or a lovely spring lunch

Serves 4

Preparation time 20 minutes, plus cooling time

Cooking time 40 minutes

4 large globe artichokes

Juice 1 lemon

1 rasher lean smoked bacon, fat stripped off and chopped

1 shallot, finely chopped

8 very fine asparagus tips (these have to be the tiny ones to fit in the artichoke cases)

1 egg, beaten

2 tbsp semi-skimmed milk

50g crumbled Gorgonzola (or your favourite blue cheese)

1 bag mixed salad leaves, tossed with some dressing, to serve

Sea salt and freshly ground pepper

Firstly, using a sharp knife trim off the artichoke stalks. Place the artichokes in a large saucepan and cover with boiling water, the lemon juice and some salt. Return to the boil, then cover and bring down to a simmer on a low heat for 25–30 minutes or until they feel tender when pierced with a sharp knife-tip. Remove from the heat and leave to cool upside down in a colander.

Meanwhile, preheat the oven to 200°C, Gas Mark 6. Fry the bacon in a hot non-stick frying pan without extra oil until crispy, adding the chopped shallots halfway through. Cook for 3–5 minutes until the shallots are softened.

Cut the asparagus tips into 3cm lengths. Blanch in boiling water for 1 minute only, then drain in a sieve and hold under cold running water for a minute or two until cool. Whisk together the eggs, milk and some seasoning.

When the artichokes are cool enough to handle, pull off the thick outer leaves (save these to eat later with a lovely low-fat French dressing). When you get to the centre, pull off the soft inner leaves, exposing the choke. Using a teaspoon, scrape off the chokes. You should have four shallow cups. Brush these lightly with oil and place on a baking tray. Trim the bases a little if needed so they sit level on the tray.

To start building up your tartlets, crumble the Gorgonzola into each base, sprinkle in the bacon and shallot mix and then scatter over the asparagus tips. Then gently spoon in the egg mix to fill them up. Bake in the oven for 10 minutes until lightly set on top and serve with the dressed salad leaves.

For a different, vegetarian option use chopped pan-fried wild mushrooms and truffle oil as a filling instead.

Tricks of the Trade

Chefs seem to be everywhere now: on the TV, in all the magazines . . .
we certainly get around. It seems that the only pre-requisite is **a love of
food and a penchant for insanity!** The food industry is very high-
energy environment but it can also be really rewarding. I'd like to think
that there is a chef in everyone – the key is just to relax and not be scared
of food, experiment and enjoy it. Everyone makes mistakes, including
me even now, so just get stuck in and have fun. Food is truly one of life's
greatest pleasures!

This chapter contains a few tricks to help you get by. A couple of
insider tips, basic shopping guidelines and suggestions on **making
your life easier**.

Basic Tomato Sauce

Serves 4

1 tbsp olive oil
1 onion, finely chopped
3 garlic cloves, finely chopped
Splash white wine
400g can chopped tomatoes
2 pinches dried oregano
1 tsp tomato purée
Salt and freshly ground black pepper
Small pinch of sugar
Handful chopped fresh basil

Heat the oil in a saucepan and sweat the onion and garlic until translucent. Add the white wine and let it bubble for 2 minutes to cook off the alcohol.

Add the tinned tomatoes, oregano, sugar and seasoning. Cover and leave to simmer for 20 minutes until thickened to a sauce. Finally, scatter in the basil and serve.

Chicken Stock

Makes about 3.5 litres/6 pints

About 1.5kg cooked or raw chicken carcasses
(and a few wings for extra flavour)
2 onions
3 carrots
4 celery sticks
2 leeks
3 garlic cloves, kept whole
1 tomato
4 parsley sprigs
2 thyme sprigs
2 bay leaves
4 whole peppercorns

Place the chicken in a very large pot – big enough to take the vegetables and water as well. Roughly chop and then wash all the vegetables, and add to the pot with the herbs, garlic and seasoning. Pour in about 6 litres/10½ pints water – enough just to cover the carcasses. Bring to the boil and then turn the heat right down. Skim off any froth or scum from the surface with a ladle. Simmer for 3–4 hours, continuing to remove any froth or fat from time to time as it comes to the surface.

Drain off and reserve the stock. Allow it to cool, then pass the liquid through a sieve to remove any remaining bits and pieces. Pour the stock into storage containers. It will keep for 2–3 days in the fridge or can be frozen for 2–3 months.

If you want to make a Thai-flavoured stock base, substitute the herbs in the basic recipe with 3 lemongrass stalks, 4 kaffir lime leaves, 1 piece of roughly chopped fresh root ginger, a piece of galangal and a bunch of chopped coriander. Finish with a good squeeze of lemon.

Flavoured Oils

Chilli Oil

Makes 500ml

8 dried chillies
1 tsp dried chilli flakes
1 rosemary sprig
500ml extra-virgin olive oil

Put the chillies, chilli flakes and rosemary in a sterilised bottle, pour in the olive oil and leave to infuse for 2 weeks in a cool, dark place before using, shaking the bottle occasionally. Remove the rosemary before using.

Ginger and Orange Oil

Makes 500ml

½ tsp coriander seeds
1 orange
5cm piece fresh root ginger
500ml light olive oil

Heat a small dry pan, then add the coriander seeds and fry them briefly until they just start to colour – this brings out their flavour. Leave to cool. Using a potato peeler, peel the zest from the orange in large strips, being careful not to take off too much white pith as this will make the oil bitter.

Cut the ginger into thin matchsticks. Put the coriander seeds, orange zest and ginger in a sterilised bottle, pour in the olive oil and leave to infuse for 3 days in a cool, dark place. Strain before using.

Garlicky Herb Oil

Makes 500ml

3 garlic cloves, lightly bashed
2 rosemary sprigs
2 thyme sprigs
½ tsp black peppercorns
3 bay leaves
500ml extra-virgin olive oil

Put all the first ingredients into a sterilised bottle, then pour in the oil. Leave to infuse for 1 week in a cool, dark place. Strain before using.

How to Cook a Lobster

In the Pot

Place the lobster(s) in the freezer for about 2 hours. Bring a pan of water to the boil – allow 3 litres per 600g–1kg lobster – and add the lobster. If cooking more than one, be careful not to overcrowd the pan. Cover with a lid and boil for about 3 minutes per 500g. This is long enough to parboil the lobster, which can then be used and cooked further in other dishes. If you want to cook the lobster completely (for example, if using for a salad), allow 4 minutes per 500g. The lobster will have turned red. Remove the lobster from the water and use accordingly.

Roasting and Grilling

Place the lobster on a secure chopping board. Pull the tail out flat. The idea is to split the lobster from head to tail down its midline, cutting through the nerve centres that run down its back to kill it instantly.

Take a large, very sharp chef's knife. Find the cross-hatch behind the lobster's head, plunge the tip of the knife right down, piercing it behind the head, then bring the rest of the knife down and through the back and tail, cutting the lobster in half. Then cut through the front of the head. You can now place the lobster on a tray and grill or roast accordingly.

How to Shop

I am a true shopaholic – not just for clothes but for food, too. I love finding new ingredients and my eyes are always bigger than my belly! Sometimes though you need some strategic planning when it comes to shopping, and I've compiled a list to help keep you stocked up with the most useful items, cutting out the unnecessary stuff.

Chefs love to use weird ingredients, but do you really need dried ancho chillies and fish paste that you use once and then have festering at the back of the cupboard? My recipes use normal ingredients that you can find in the supermarket.

If you keep your 'foodie wardrobe' stocked, you can make a fab meal anytime! One important tip: don't shop when you're hungry – you will only come back with a basketful of instantly consumable foods like crisps and cheese, which will then be devoured in the car park. OK, ladies, here we go . . .

Food Wardrobe

Dried Goods

Baking powder

Bicarbonate of soda

Buckwheat

Cornflour

Dark chocolate (the darker the better)

Dried fruit
  apricots, prunes, dates, sultanas and cherries

Dried nuts
  pistachios, almonds, hazelnuts, pecans,
  desiccated coconut, pine nuts, unsalted
  peanuts, walnuts

Dried porcini mushrooms

Flour
  self-raising, plain, wholemeal

Gelatine leaves

Lentils
  red and puy

Noodles
  buckwheat, rice, egg

Oatcakes (for recipe see page 74)

Oatmeal

Onions
  shallots, red onion, white onion

Pasta
  penne, tagliatelle, linguine (wheat-free if you
  need it. Kamut pasta is a very good wheat-free
  pasta)

Polenta

Quinoa

Rice
  brown, Basmati, Thai jasmine, risotto

Rye crisp breads

Sea salt crystals (Maldon salt is great and widely
sold)

Sugar
  Fruit sugar, caster, icing (royal and normal),
light brown, palm sugar

Stock cubes or powder
  chicken and vegetable (Marigold is a great
brand)

Herbs and Spices

There are two types of herbs: soft and hard. The soft herbs (including tarragon, basil, parsley, dill and coriander) need to be used when fresh. Hard herbs are great used fresh too, but are also fantastic when used dried, they include rosemary, thyme, oregano and sage. Here's my list of good dried herbs and spices to keep in stock:

Bay leaves
Cardamom pods
Cayenne pepper
Chilli flakes
Chilli powder
Chinese five spice
Cinnamon
Cumin seeds and ground cumin
Curry powder
Dried oregano (this is the only herb that I think is actually better when dried)
Dried rosemary
Dried thyme

Freshly ground black pepper
Garam Masala
Garlic cloves
Garlic powder
Ground coriander
Mixed spice
Saffron
Smoked paprika
Star anise
Turmeric
Whole nutmeg

Oils and Liquids

Balsamic vinegar
Cassis liqueur
Cider
Dark soy sauce
Extra virgin olive oil (the best quality you can afford)
Hoisin sauce
Light soy sauce
Lighter olive oil for cooking
Mirin (rice wine)
Oyster sauce
Port

Sesame seed oil
Sweet chilli sauce
Tabasco
Thai fish sauce
Truffle oil
Vanilla extract
Walnut oil
Wine – red and white
Wine vinegar – red and white, and rice wine vinegar
Worchester sauce

Jars, Bottles and Cans

Anchovies

Artichokes, pre-prepared and stored in olive oil

Boneless and skinless salmon in spring water

Capers

Chickpeas

Chopped tomatoes

Chutney

Coconut milk (low fat)

Dijon mustard

English mustard

Hot horseradish

Ketchup (reduced sugar, if possible)

Low-sugar raspberry jam

Mango chutney

Maple syrup

Olives

Peeled chestnuts

Pickled pink ginger

Red onion marmalade

Roasted peeled peppers

Runny honey

Salted capers (need to be washed before using)

Sweet corn

Tandoori paste

Thai curry paste

Tomato passata

Tomato purée

Tuna in spring water

Wasabi paste

White beans

Wholegrain mustard

Fridge Savers

Here are some fresh ingredients that I use a lot in my cooking – if you have just a few on hand in your fridge you'll be able to throw together something fabulous on the go in a matter of moments.

Asparagus

Avocado

Basil

Butternut squash

Carrot

Chives

Chorizo

Coriander

Courgette

Crème fraîche (low-fat)

Cucumber

Feta (half-fat)

Flat-leaf parsley

Free-range eggs

Fresh ginger

Goats' cheese

Greek yogurt (0% fat)

Lean smoked bacon

Lemon

Lemongrass

Lime

Mozzarella

Parma ham

Parmesan cheese

Peppers

Red chillies

Skimmed milked

Spring onions

Sweet potato

Freezer Savers

Broad beans

Filo pastry sheets

Homemade pesto

Petit pois

Prawns

Summer fruits

Dressing Up

When I say dressing up, I mean the table, not you, but it's all part of being a Glamorous Gourmet. Here are some suggestions on making the table look gorgeous without spending too much cash and some little tips on cheap ways to serve canapés.

For your fab little canapé soirées and afternoon teas

- Mirror tiles and slate tiles – very cheap from any hardware store. Canapés look extremely chic served on them.
- Candle trays and little wooden trays – Habitat do some good ones for canapés. They're cheap and can always be reused for their original purpose.
- Bamboo steamers, sushi platters and Chinese soup spoons all add a fun vibe when serving Asian foods.

Making Your Table Beautiful

- Decorate around your canapés with flower heads bought cheaply at the supermarket or your local flower stall. If you just use the heads, it doesn't matter if the stems aren't perfect.
- Tea lights are cheap and look brilliant scattered across tables.
- Sequins, plastic jewels, feathers and ribbon can always be bought cheaply and used wherever inspiration takes you. Either scatter across the table or wrap the ribbon and feathers around glasses and cutlery.
- Whenever you get chance, have a look in charity stores for pretty and mismatched crockery, so you build up your own tea party set.
- Finally, use shot glasses for serving mini jellies and soup shots.

TRICKS OF THE TRADE

Seasonal Suggestions

Spring

- Think yellows and pale greens: Daffodils, tulips and bluebells are ideal flowers to use.
- Use some duck eggs in your cooking. Hollow out the shells and keep for salt and pepper pots.
- Pastel-coloured ribbons and silks are good here.
- For Easter buy bags of mini eggs and colourful foil-covered eggs. Pop these in bowls – people can help themselves and they also act as a cute decoration.
- Use different types of eggcups to sit flower heads in or for serving mini puddings.

Summer

- I use shells that I have collected from beaches on my travels as a centrepiece, along with pieces of sea glass and beach wood.
- For flowers, I use dusky English roses and lilies for daytime affairs and deep fuchsia Indian summer pinks and purples in the evenings.
- Again thinking of the Indian hot summer theme, I use gold threads and gold-embellished candleholders.

Autumn

- Think reds, oranges and yellows for flowers.
- I use large golden leaves for coasters or mats in the centre of the table.
- Simple touches such as bowls of apples and pears and smaller bowls of blackberries look pretty too.

Winter

- Whites and crystals look lovely – think snowy winter wonderlands. Add some red berries through bowls of cranberries or large branches of holly heavy with red berries for contrast.
- Mistletoe and ivy are cheap and cheerful.
- Cinnamon sticks, clove-studded oranges and mandarins are old favourites too.

Great Shops for Decorations and Serving Bits and Bobs

- B&Q: good for mirror and slate tiles.
- Charity chops: miss-matched crockery or, if you can afford it, look in antique shops for special pieces.
- Habitat: candle platters to be used for canapés and tea parties.
- Heals: lots of pretty candles. They also have a great kitchen section that can work out being much cheaper than you think. I bought a fun and practical set of pink baking trays and cake tins from there.
- Marks and Spencer: fantastic for Easter eggs and flowers too.
- Tesco: really good value for money. Tesco has some brilliant pieces for the kitchen and home. Also great for flowers.
- Wedgwood and Thomas Goode: beautiful plates and serving platters, but are at the higher end of the market.
- Zara Home: über-pretty selection of plates, tea-light holders, glasses and cutlery. Also good for throws and cushions.

Great Shops for Kitchen Equipment

And finally, here are a few names to drop when shopping for kitchen equipment. The list is endless really so here are just a few of my favourites.

- Bosch: very good ovens and dishwashers.
- Braun: I have used my trusty handheld stick blender for years for all my soups, sauces, pesto etc.
- DeLonghi: great for coffee machine, kettles etc.
- KitchenAid: brilliant for blenders, mixers and bigger kitchen pieces.
- Le Creuset pots and pans: my mother has always used them and they are simply fab.
- Professional kitchen tongs are essential.
- Slipmat baking sheets.
- Wusthof knives: the Culinair range is my favourite.

Page 10: Dress, ISSA; earrings, Le Merola; bracelet, SHO
Page 12: Shirt, Tomas Pink; skirt, Joseph; watch, Sophie's own
Page 46: Top, Joseph; tracksuit bottoms, N.PEAL; watch, Sophie's own
Page 78: As page 10
Page 154: Dress, Ashley Isham; earrings, Le Merola; bracelet, Le Merola
Page 176: Dress on Sophie, Velvet; dress held up in mirror by Sophie, Ben de Lisi
Page 202: Top, Joseph; jeans, J Brand; sandals, Giuseppe Zanotti; watch, Sophie's own
Page 224: Dress, Diane Von Furstenberg; bracelets both Merola

Stock list
Ashley Isham, 02074999658, www.asleyisham.com
Ben de Lisi, 02077302994, www.bendelisi.com
Diane Von Furstenberg, 02074990886, www.dvflondon.com
Giuseppe Zanotti 02075913900, www.giuseppi-zanotti-design.com
ISSA, 02073524243, www.issalondon.com
Joseph, 02076108441, www.joseph.co.uk
La Merola, 02073519338, www.merola.co.uk
N.PEAL, 02074996485, www.npeal.com
SHO, 02073832772, www.shojewellery.com
Trilogy, 02077306515, www.trilogystores.co.uk
Velvet, 02075808644, www.velvet-tees.com

Styling by Mary-Anna Kearney
Hair and make-up by Michelle Foxley

Index

A

afternoon tea 145–52, 213
aioli, lemon 158
alcoholic drinks 86–7, 122–6
anchovy and red pepper salad 36
angel cakes 147, 149
apples 15, 97, 124
apricots, spiced poached 144
artichokes 59, 200
Asian food 22–3, 32–3, 194
asparagus 200
    and prawns with lemon aioli 158
    roasted 162–3
    Serrano- and goat's cheese-wrapped 94
aubergine 62, 106–8
autumn 215
avocado
    butter 179
    crostinis 120
    salsa 198–9

B

bacon, crispy, feta hotcakes with 142–3
Balinese food 32–3, 186
bananas
    and macadamia bread with blueberries 139
    strudel 67
basil and white peach Bellinis 126
beans
    broad 25
    Mexican 136
    white bean crush 170
    white bean and truffle soup 34
beef
    grilled rib eye with chimchirri dressing 19
    Neeps- and tatties-topped cottage pie 50–1
    rare roast, with truffle oil and Parmesan 91
    stifado 49
Bellinis 124, 126
biscotti, macadamia nut and lemon 66
blood oranges 113, 162–3
Bloody Marys 86–7, 123, 131
blueberries
    Banana and macadamia bread with 138

Pavlova with lemon fromage frais and 151
raspberry and nectarine with a rosewater sabayon 68–9
    and sloe gin sauce 24
bok choi 16
bread
    banana and macadamia 139
    homemade soda 138
brioche 103
broccoli, chilli and garlic 193
brunch 137–44
burgers
    my big fat Greek 20
    superfood 135
butternut squash
    and almond risotto 56–7
    Dolcelatte and rocket wraps 41
    and orange and ginger soup 189
    roasted 162–3

C

cabbage, wilted Savoy 104–5
cakes
    flourless hazelnut 197
    little angel cakes 147, 149
    refrigerator 160–1
calves' liver with caramelised shallots, Gorgonzola and roasted artichokes 59
canapés 80–94, 213
caponata stuffed tomatoes 106–8
Caprioskas 125
carpaccio, sesame-crusted tuna 195
carrots 170, 187
cauliflower purée 92–3
celeriac 24
    gratin 104–5
champagne 37, 122, 124, 145
chargrilled recipes 187, 193
cheesecakes, vanilla, with cassis and blackcurrant compote 152
cherries, sour 54
chestnuts 31, 103
chicken
    chargrilled fennel chicken on courgette and carrot 187
    chicken liver paté with Armagnac prunes 98–9
    coronation chicken patties with mango chutney mayo 81
    ginger and hoison lettuce wraps 44

marinated pieces 75
Parmesan crispy chicken with tomato, avocado and sweetcorn salsa 198–9
poached chicken and Asian coleslaw 194
quinoa with tandoori chicken 184–5
shitake and smoked chicken broth 96
stock 205
Thai chicken soup 182
thyme and cider pot-roasted chicken 52–3
vine-leaf wrapped chicken with ricotta, pine nut and mint stuffing 110–11
chilli 73, 206
Chinese food 16, 92–3, 96
chips
polenta 60–1
sweet potato 19
chives 132–3
chocolate 160–1
jasmine pots 116–17
Salted chocolate caramel éclairs 148–50
sauce 67
chorizo
pan-fried 131
and smoked monkfish 168–9
chowder, Thai sweet corn and sweet potato 58
chutney, cumin, feta and mango 102
cider 28, 52–3
cocktails 86–7, 122–6
coconut and lime surprise pudding 70–1
cod, salt 140–1
cod 186
coleslaw, Asian 194
compote
cassis and blackcurrant 152
rhubarb 64–5
cottage pie, neeps- and tatties-topped 50–1
courgettes 40, 187
crab omelette, Asian 22–3
Cranachan parfait 172
crème brûlée 112
crisps, pita 73, 76–7
crostinis, sourdough, avocado and sweet chilli 120
crumble, summer fruit and pear 35
cucumber cups with wasabi tuna tartare 82–3
cumin 102, 170
cupboard essentials 209–11

D

dates, fried eggs with 121
desserts 35, 63–71, 112–17, 160–1, 172–5, 197
detox food 188–95
diet food 176–87

dietary restrictions 26–7, 74, 196–201
dinner parties 95–117
dips, pink peppercorn and nectarine 94
Dolcelatte, rocket and roast squash wraps 41
dressings
chimchirri 19
Niçoise 29
pomegranate and blood orange 162–3
soy and mustard 195
duck
roasted, with star anise pears 109
and sour cherry ragu with buttered noodles 54

E

Easter 215
éclairs, salted chocolate caramel 148–50
egg dishes
fried eggs with dates 121
masala eggs with cooling coriander yoghurt 134
my comforting kedgeree 130
Nasi Goreng 32–3
salt cod Brandade eggs Benedict 140–1
elderflower 124

F

family dinners 167–71
fennel 29, 138, 187
feta 38–9, 73, 102, 142–3
figs
little live-bites of fig, almond and honey 160–1
mozzarella with fig and Parma ham 166
spiced poached apricots and 144
fish
Balinese spiced fish with coconut rice 186
Grilled polenta with red pepper and anchovy salad 36
My comforting kedgeree 130
Salt cod Brandade eggs Benedict 140–1
Sardines on peppernata 183
Sea bass on roasted fennel with Niçoise dressing 29
see also mackerel; monkfish; salmon
five-spice pork chops 16
Florida food 26–7
flowers 213, 215
fridge/freezer essentials 212
frittatas, courgette, onion and green olive 40
fromage frais, lemon 151

G

garlic sauce 15
garlicky herb oil 206

ginger 44, 112, 146, 149, 189, 206
goat's cheese-wrapped asparagus 94
Gorgonzola 59, 200
Greek food 15, 20, 38–9, 49, 110–11

H

haddock 130
hangover cures 127–36
hazelnut cake, flourless 197
herbs 210
hollandaise sauce 140–1
honey 55, 142–3, 160–1
hummus with pomegranates and pine nuts 76–7

I

Indian food 114–15, 134, 184–5
Italian food 56–7, 60–2

J

Jasmine chocolate pots 116–17
jellies
    blood orange and grenadine 113
    passion-fruit 146, 149

K

kedgeree, my comforting 130
kitchen equipment 216
kohlrabi 109

L

lamb
    fillet, with white bean crush and cumin carrots 170
    and Greek salad pitas 38–9
    honey- and lavender- glazed, with potato gratin 55
    rack, with caponata stuffed tomatoes and olive oil mash 106–8
    Sardinian stew, with polenta chips 60–1
leeks 28
lemon 66, 151, 158, 171
lemongrass, chilli and kaffir lime leaf Collins 126–7
lentils, caramelised onion, and brown rice with Greek yoghurt 192
Lime and coconut surprise pudding 70–1
liver, calves' 59
lobster 207
linguine 157
lychee salad 112
lycopene 131

M

macadamias 66, 138

mackerel
    curried potted, with apple salad 97
    with garlic sauce and apple and walnut salad 15
mains
    comfort food 48–62
    dietary restrictions 198–200
    dinner party 103–11
    family dinners 167–71
    from the store cupboard 30–6
    quick fix 14–29
    romantic 155–9, 162–3
Manchego, membrillo and Serrano ham skewers 88
Mandarin Caprioskas 125
mango 81, 89, 119
marinades
    chilli, lemongrass and coconut 75
    maple syrup, chilli, rosemary 75
    saffron, lemon and garlic 75
mash
    olive oil 106–8
    white bean 170
mayo, mango chutney 81
Melanzane Parmigiana 62
Mexican beans 136
miso salmon with black-sesame pickled vegetables and steamed rice 180–1
miso seafood soup 190–1
monkfish
    crispy, cauliflower purée, and wild mushrooms 92–3
    smoked, on sweet potato and chorizo 168–9
mozzarella with fig and Parma ham 166
mushrooms 92–3
    portabello mushrooms with chestnut duxelle and brioche 103
    shitake and smoked chicken broth 96

N

Nasi Goreng 32–3
nectarines 68–9, 94
Neeps- and tatties-topped cottage pie 50–1
Niçoise dressing 29
noodles 54
Novelli, Jean Christophe 55

O

oatcakes, homemade 74
oils 210
    flavoured 206
omelette, Asian crab 22–3
oysters
    Bloody Mary oyster shots 86–7
    Oysters Romanoff 159

P

packed lunches 37–44
panacotta, Greek yoghurt, with rhubarb compote 64–5
pancakes 142
Parma ham 25, 166
Parmesan 91, 198–9
passion-fruit jellies with white chocolate cream and ginger
shortbreads 146, 149
pasta
    lobster linguine 157
    penne arrabiatta 165
paté, chicken liver 98–9
pavlova with lemon fromage frais and blueberries 151
peach 126
peanuts 84–5
pears 35, 109
peas 25
penne arrabiatta 165
peppercorns, pink 94
peppernata, sardines on 183
peppers 36
Persian food 121
pesto 106–8
pie, Neeps- and tatties-topped cottage 50–1
pine nuts 76–7
pink peppercorns 94
pitas
    crisps 73, 76–7
    lamb and Greek salad 38–9
plum, cinnamon and sour cream tart 174–5
polenta
    chips 60–1
    grilled 36
pomegranates 76–7, 162–3
pork
    five-spice chops with garlicky greens 16
    peanut and coriander salad cups 84–5
potatoes
    cottage pie 50–1
    gratin 55
    olive oil mash 106–8
    ravigote 42–3
prawns
    and asparagus with lemon aioli 158
    Ceviche 100–1
    Nasi Goreng 32–3
prunes, Armagnac 98–9

Q

quail on roasted butternut squash and asparagus with
pomegranate and blood orange dressing 162–3
quinoa with tandoori chicken 184–5

R

rarebit, glam gourmet 90
raspberry, nectarine and blueberry with a rosewater sabayon
68–9
redcurrants 104–5
refrigerator cakes 160–1
rhubarb compote 64–5
rib eye, grilled 19
rice dishes
    fish-based 32–3, 130, 180–1, 186
    pork-based 16
    vegetarian 31, 56–7, 192
rice pudding moulds, cardamom and rose water 114–15
ricotta 110–11, 132–3
risotto
    butternut squash and almond 56–7
    chestnut and porcini 31
rocket 41

S

sabayon, rosewater 68–9
salad
    apple 97
    apple and walnut 15
    Greek 38–9
    lychee 112
    pork, peanut and coriander cups 84–5
    red pepper and anchovy 36
    tzatziki 20
salmon
    blackened-salmon and mango tartlets 89
    brown sugar and Pernod-cured salmon with fennel shavings
    and homemade soda bread 138
    chive French toast with smoked salmon and ricotta 132–3
    miso salmon with black-sesame pickled vegetables and
    steamed rice 180–1
    poached, and ravigote potatoes 42–3
salsa, tomato, avocado and sweetcorn 198–9
samosas, cumin feta and mango chutney 102
sardines on peppernata 183
sauces
    basic tomato 205
    blueberry and sloe gin 24
    chocolate 67
    garlic 15
    hollandaise 140–1
scallop and shrimp tacos 26–7
sea bass on roasted fennel with Niçoise dressing 29
seafood 26–7, 32–3, 100–1, 157–8, 190–1, 207
seasonal ideas 215
Serrano ham 88, 94

shallots, caramelised 59
shopping 208–12, 216
shortbread, white chocolate cream and ginger 146, 149
shrimp and scallop tacos 26–7
smoothies, mango, lime and coconut 119
snacks 72–6, 118–21, 164–6
soda bread, homemade 138
soup
    butternut squash, orange and ginger 189
    miso seafood 190–1
    Shitake and smoked chicken 96
    Somerset cider and leek 28
    Thai chicken 182
    Thai sweet corn and sweet potato 58
    white bean and truffle 34
spices 210
springtime 215
starters 96–102
stews 49, 60–1
stock, chicken 205
strudel, banana 67
stuffing, ricotta, pine nut and mint 110–11
sugar 63
summertime 215
sweet potatoes
    baked, with avocado butter 179
    chips 19
    smoked monkfish on 168–9
and Thai sweet corn chowder 58
sweetcorn 58, 198–9
swordfish 186

table decorations 213–16
tacos, scallop and shrimp 26–7
tartlets, blackened-salmon and mango 89
tarts
    low-carb 200
    plum, cinnamon and sour cream 174–5
Thai food 58, 85, 182
toast
chive French toast with smoked salmon and ricotta 132–3
pan-fried chorizo, cherry tomatoes and chillies on 131
tomatoes
    basic tomato sauce 205
    caponata stuffed 106–8
    lobster linguine 157
    pan-fried chorizo, cherry tomatoes and chillies on toast 131
    penne arrabiatta 165
    relish 20, 134
trifle, tropical 173
truffles 25, 34, 91
tuna

    cucumber cups with wasabi tuna tartare 82–3
    sesame-crusted carpaccio, with soy and mustard dressing 195
turkey
    chargrilled steaks with chilli and garlic broccoli 193
    superfood burger 135
tzatziki 20, 39

veal rolls with lemon and olives 171
vegetarian dishes
    light bites 90, 134, 136
    mains 31, 56–7, 103, 165, 192
    soups 34, 189
    starters 102
venison
    redcurrant glazed, with celeriac gratin and wilted Savoy cabbage 104–5
steak with blueberry and sloe gin sauce 24
vine-leaf wrapped chicken with ricotta, pine nut and mint stuffing 110–11

wasabi Bloody Mary 123
wine 122
winter 215
wraps
    chicken, ginger and hoison lettuce 44
    roast squash, Dolcelatte, and rocket 41

yogurt
    cooling coriander 134
    Greek yogurt panacotta with rhubarb compote 64–5